WHY STRAIGHT WOMEN LOVE GAY ROMANCE

GEOFFREY KNIGHT
EDITED BY KRIS JACEN

mlrpress
www.mlrpress.com

Copyright 2012 by Geoffrey Knight

Published by
MLR Press, LLC
3052 Gaines Waterport Rd.
Albion, NY 14411

Visit ManLoveRomance Press, LLC on the Internet:
www.mlrpress.com

Cover Art by Michael Cunningham
Editing by Kris Jacen

Print format: ISBN# 978-1-60820-762-6
ebook format: ISBN#978-1-60820-763-3

Issued 2012

One of the world's biggest secrets is coming out…Why do straight women love gay romance?

What is it that attracts straight women to the idea of two men falling in love? Is it the muscles? The mystery of the male mind? The idea of true love overcoming all odds? How has it changed who these women are and how they see the world? And how powerful is this once-silent army of readers in the fight for equality?

Readers, authors, publishers and editors share their opinions and tell some very personal stories that will make you laugh, cry and ultimately inspire, as 32 women across 9 countries and 4 continents—including New York Times bestselling author Suzanne Brockmann, Amelia from the Huffington Post, bestselling gay romance author Carol Lynne and award-winning publisher and author Laura Baumbach—finally reveal…

Why Straight Women Love Gay Romance.

Featuring a roll call of some of the best writers of gay erotica and mysteries today!

Derek Adams	Z. Allora	Maura Anderson
Simone Anderson	Victor J. Banis	Laura Baumbach
Helen Beattie	Ally Blue	J.P. Bowie
Barry Brennessel	Nowell Briscoe	Jade Buchanan
James Buchanan	TA Chase	Charlie Cochrane
Karenna Colcroft	Michael G. Cornelius	Jamie Craig
Ethan Day	Diana DeRicci	Vivien Dean
Taylor V. Donovan	Theo Fenraven	S.J. Frost
Kimberly Gardner	Michael Gouda	Kaje Harper
Alex Ironrod	AC Katt	Thomas Kearnes
Sasha Keegan	Kiernan Kelly	K-lee Klein
Geoffrey Knight	Christopher Koehler	Matthew Lang
J.L. Langley	Vincent Lardo	Cameron Lawton
Anna Lee	Elizabeth Lister	Clare London
William Maltese	Z.A. Maxfield	Timothy McGivney
Tere Michaels	AKM Miles	Robert Moore
Reiko Morgan	Jet Mykles	William Neale
N.J. Nielsen	Cherie Noel	Gregory L. Norris
Willa Okati	Erica Pike	Neil S. Plakcy
Rick R. Reed	A.M. Riley	AJ Rose
Rob Rosen	George Seaton	Riley Shane
Jardonn Smith	DH Starr	Richard Stevenson
Liz Strange	Marshall Thornton	Lex Valentine
Haley Walsh	Mia Watts	Lynley Wayne
Missy Welsh	Ryal Woods	Stevie Woods
Lance Zarimba	Mark Zubro	

Check out titles, both available and forthcoming, at
www.mlrpress.com

For Helen,

Who made me realize there was a world of female readers out there.

And for Bill Neale,

Who made me realize this book needed to be written.

THE AGENDA
TABLE OF CONTENTS

ACKNOWLEDGMENTS

There's a saying that no book is written by one person alone, and it's especially true of this one. The thirty-two women interviewed in this book not only said 'yes' when I approached them to be part of the project, they were thrilled to be involved and eager to have their voices heard. Without their honesty and openness, this book would never have been possible, so ladies... thank you one and all!

I also want to say a special thanks to Laura Baumbach, my publisher, who made this project a labor of love the moment I pitched the concept to her. Thanks also to Kris Jacen who helped me take every step of this journey, from sharing ideas all the way through to editing what was quite a large project and bringing it back to something short, sharp, and concise. Thanks also to my dear friend Michael Cunningham for designing a cover that is sexy, eye-catching, and ready to spark any reader's curiosity.

And last but by no means least, a truly heartfelt thanks to Suzanne Brockmann who embraced this project from the very start and poured her time, experience and love into it.

I hope that together we've started a discussion that will have the whole world talking... and acting... and changing the way we all think.

PROLOGUE
WHO? WHAT? WHY?

Here's how it all started. I was having a few drinks with friends and when one of them asked how my writing was going, I mentioned that I'd just finished a new manuscript and had sent it off to my friend Helen to read. The conversation went something like this—

> Friend at the pub: "Helen? A woman reads your books?"

> Geoff: "Yeah, lots of women read my books. In fact, the majority of my readers are female."

> Friend at pub (curious): "But I thought you only wrote gay porn?"

> Geoff: "Well, it's a bit more than just porn. But it's erotica and romance, and yes, it's gay."

> Friend at pub (perplexed): "What are lesbians doing reading about gay men?"

> Geoff: "I don't think there are that many lesbians who read my books, maybe a few, who knows."

> Friend at pub (getting really confused now): "But you said women read your books."

> Geoff: "Yeah, mostly straight women."

> Friend at pub (downright baffled): "But… why?"

> Geoff (searching but not coming up with much): "I don't know."

That was the first, but by no means the last time I've ever had that discussion. In fact, it's a conversation that's come up at readings and book club appearances and writer's forums that I've attended in both Australia and the United States. And every single time, the discussion plays out exactly the same way, with the exception of the last chat I had on the subject which ended with—

> Geoff (searching but not coming up with
>   much): "I don't know. But you know what?
>   I'm gonna find out!"

And so it began.

I started thinking about how to get to the bottom of this, who to go to for answers, and whether people were ready to know about something that was, in my opinion, one of the world's best kept secrets—Why do straight women love gay romance?

I had met a great number of wonderful women at the inaugural GayRomLit retreat in New Orleans in October 2011 (and yes, the overwhelming majority of attendees were straight women), so I knew I could comfortably ask several friends I'd made at GRL if they'd like to help out. There were also a great number of women on Facebook and several Yahoo Groups dedicated to gay romance who I thought might be interested. I started contemplating the kind of questions I wanted to ask—

> How did you discover gay romance?
>
> Who knows you read it?
>
> What reaction do you get when you tell
>   people?
>
> Does your husband know?
>
> Has it changed your sex life?

—but in the back of my mind one lingering thought kept holding me back.

What if these women didn't want their secret
   told?

What if they were happy reading about gay
   men in love, without the world even knowing about it?

Then in March 2012, something else happened that made
me want to push past this barrier. A wonderful gay romance
author named William Neale died. Bill wrote some of the most
touching, honest, and heartfelt gay love stories ever written. One
day he sent his latest manuscript to his publisher. The next day he
was gone, without any warning at all.

News of his death took this very small and very tight little gay
romance community by complete surprise. Bill had made many
friends and fans, he was one of the organizers of GayRomLit,
and his passing left us all reeling, whether we knew him well or
not.

And this was something I couldn't figure out either.

I barely knew Bill. I spoke to him a few times at the retreat in
New Orleans and via email, and yet his death left me devastated.
And I wasn't the only one. Fellow authors and fans of Bill who
had never met him were left so upset by his sudden passing that
it were as though they'd lost a member of their own family.

In fact, the subject line of the email that Bill's publisher, Laura
Baumbach, sent out was: A Death in the Family.

It was a few days later, after thinking about Bill almost non-
stop, that I realized how powerful Laura's subject line was, how
true it was, and this was why we were all so devastated.

Because we are a family.

We shared something that the world didn't know about.

Together we all loved gay romance. Together we shared a
passion for stories about the love between two men.

When the attendees of that first GayRomLit retreat in
October 2011 all came together for the first time, it was like being
in a safe place, sharing something other people didn't know or

understand. It was like being with family, despite the fact that we were all pretty much strangers. There was a sense of courage, of confidence, of unspoken understanding, as though so many people there were "coming out" in their own way, for the first time. There was instant trust, an instant friendship between us all.

Then Bill died and we lost one of our own.

And all I could think was: the world needs to know we're here!

How can someone like Bill die and his wonderful words and stories be loved and cherished by so few?

I truly believed it was time for this secret—these stories—to be told.

The first thing I did was send an email to Laura and my editor, Kris, at MLR Press and explain how I felt, what I wanted to do. With their undying determination, passion, and years of experience publishing gay romance, Laura and Kris whole-heartedly backed the project.

The second thing I did was approach the friends I had made at GayRomLit as well as online. I also approached some women I had never spoken to before, strangers who have since become my friends. I told them I wanted their personal stories, their honest answers to some very private questions. To be honest, I wasn't at all sure what kind of reaction I was going to get, but when I got it, it blew me away. Almost all the women I approached not only wanted to be a part of this book, they were genuinely thrilled and excited and passionate to help.

Yes, these women have something to say!

Initially I asked eight women to participate. Their responses had me captivated. They introduced me to theories and thoughts on the subject I hadn't even imagined. I was hooked, and so I asked four more women. Then another five. And still I wanted to know more. I wasn't simply fascinated by their responses; I was spellbound!

In the end, I interviewed thirty-two women from nine countries across four continents. And their answers are as diverse as they are riveting, which thrilled me because diversity was one of my main goals with this project.

I wanted the award-winning publisher and the #1 New York Times bestselling author, as well as the most prolific and successful female writers in this category. But I also wanted the fans, the women who read gay romance not with aspirations of writing a novel, but just for their love of these books.

I wanted women from different age groups in all kinds of different relationships. I wanted grandmothers and soccer moms and single women of all ages. I wanted the happily married and the happily divorced. I wanted women with children both gay and straight, as well as those who have no intention of ever raising a family.

And I wanted cultural diversity. From a town in Iceland to America's Deep South; from mainland China where homosexuality was classed as a mental illness until as recently as 2001, to Germany where the Mayor of Berlin is openly gay; from Italy to Ireland; from Australia to Canada; from Hong Kong to England.

What I found were stories that made me laugh, cry, and shake my head in astonishment. But what I also found was something that truly astounded me. I found a once-silent army of women who, simply through their love of gay romance, have become an army fighting for equality. They're educating their husbands and children. They're changing the perceptions of their parents and friends and work colleagues. They're joining support groups and waving flags and becoming a true force to be reckoned with. Before they started reading gay romance, many of these women didn't even have any gay friends. Now they are one of the strongest, and most surprising, waves of support for equal rights on the planet—and most of the world, both gay and straight, doesn't even know it.

Well all that's about to change.

It's time to meet the ladies.

◆   ◆   ◆

REDEFINING NORMAL
BY SUZANNE BROCKMANN

This year marks the tenth anniversary of the first time that my son Jason was told by a stranger that he was an abomination, and was better off dead.

He was sixteen years old when it happened, attending an equal marriage rally in downtown Boston. He encountered some anti-gay religious zealots with signs that said, "God hates you." And one of the women holding one of those ugly signs told my precious baby, directly to his sweet face, that he was better off dead.

Better off dead.

I am a writer, and I have a hefty imagination. I have to confess that over the past ten years, I have kicked that woman's ass to hell and back in every conceivable way.

But here's the thing: Although the outrage-inspired self-righteous fantasy is fun to play out in my mind, the *truth* is that this battle for equal rights that I'm fighting, this war of ideas and ideals, of beliefs and values, is not going to be won with bitchslaps and violence.

No, this is a fight that can be won, and *will* be won, through heartfelt framing and powerful words.

And I'll say it again: *I am a writer.*

Which means that as nice as it would have felt to shout, "Suck it, bitch!" as I threw an elbow jab into that hater's nose, I knew I could best protect my son and my LGBT friends by using my wordsmithing skills to do something more important, something even better.

I could help redefine normal.

I could write stories and create characters who subtly, subconsciously change the way in which people view this world that we live in.

And I have.

It's possible you don't know me, so before I go any further, let me introduce myself. My name is Suz Brockmann. And since I was first published back in 1993, I've written fifty-one books in which the primary focus was on two people who connect, spark, and fall in love. But for far longer than I've been a published romance author, since 1985 in fact, I've been the fiercely proud mother of a really terrific gay son.

I was pretty certain that Jason was gay as early as 1988, when he was around three years old. And I was *absolutely* certain, whatever his sexual orientation might be, that he was brilliantly, *beautifully* perfect exactly as he was.

I never had a moment of doubt about that.

But I was deeply concerned about the fact that my precious child was going to grow up and live in a world that could, at least at times, be hostile and unfriendly to LGBT people. And as my eyes were opened to what it meant to live in America as a gay person, I became even more concerned.

I discovered to my dismay that a high school student hears an average of twenty-five gay slurs in the course of a single day. And the statistics about LGBT teens who attempted suicide were terrifying. Why *did* so many LGBT kids try to kill themselves?

Keeping in mind those twenty-five slurs a day, it wasn't that hard to figure out.

Back in the 1980s and '90s, most gay kids (and I believe this holds true for today, at least in some parts of this gigantic red/blue/purple country) grew up feeling different and isolated and alone--mostly because all of the other gay kids were hiding, too. These sensitive, vulnerable kids are often told over and *over* that being gay is bad and wrong, and that *they* are bad and wrong--not just by the brainwashing delivered by other kids while at school, but also by family and friends and teachers and religious leaders.

At worst, the message is overt. But even when it's not, the message is there, in the implied condemnation given when parents, teachers, and role models *don't* talk openly and respectfully about LGBT family, friends, and community members. Oftentimes, it's ringingly clear in the subtext of messages meant to encourage: "No girlfriend yet? Cheer up, kiddo. Once you get to college the girls will be all over you." Message: Being gay is not an option.

And when being gay is not an option for kids who fear rejection, whose own self-rejection and self-loathing is growing and *growing*, suicide too often becomes an alternative.

Yeah, it's pretty easy math.

Still, back in 1988, I took a deep breath and I vowed that my kid was going to grow up knowing and *believing* what I believed: that he was perfect, exactly the way he was.

My mission statement as Jason's parent was to make sure that Jason knew that *being gay was an option.*

My husband, Ed, and I quickly developed strategies of support, strategies that we put into place back when Jason was still tiny. We made a point to remove social stereotyping from our daily lives. Boys could play with dolls and girls could play with cars because kids were kids and toys were toys. Who wants to take ballet lessons? Who wants to play soccer? Everything was open wide to both of our kids.

We always used gender neutral language. "Someday you'll meet the person with whom you'll want to spend the rest of your life!"

We tried our best to make sure that Jason never felt isolated or different or wrong. We were lucky because Jason loved theatre, and was a very talented actor from a ridiculously early age. From the time that he was eight years old, we drove him endlessly to rehearsals and performances because we knew, at least in the Venn diagram of life in Boston, the gay community and the theatre community had a very large intersection. So Jace grew up with a huge number of really terrific gay role models at the Turtle Lane Playhouse in Newton—and, bonus, we made some wonderful friends along the way, too.

We had a house rule that was strictly adhered to by all of our family and friends: No gay slurs or gay jokes!

We had the ability, thanks to my success as a novelist, to put Jason in a really funky-but-wonderful alternative private school where he wasn't exposed to daily gay bashing, where respect for others was the primary rule.

And most of all, we made sure that Jason knew we loved him, unconditionally and always.

We did everything but roll out a red carpet for him, and he *still* didn't say the words, "Mom, I'm gay," until he was fifteen. And talking to him about it, all these years later, he's admitted that he was nervous about telling us.

Because even though we tried our best to give him the message that being gay was an option, society was telling him otherwise.

It shouldn't be that way.

Things are changing and—at least in the world of romance fiction—I've tried my best to do my part.

During those years I was not only working to raise a healthy, happy, self-confident and secure gay son, but I was also writing mainstream romantic fiction full-time. And early on in my career, I paid close attention to how gay people were portrayed not just in the world of romance novels, but in pop culture; in all fiction--on TV, in movies, and in books.

For years, the gay character was the bad guy. The serial killer. (*Silence of the Lambs*, right? Yikes.)

But then--happily--the gay character took on the role of the witty sidekick. Gay men became the best friend and confident of the female main character. But their participation in the story tended to remain stereotypical. They were hairdressers or interior decorators and they swept into scenes like a hurricane of wit. They redecorated the apartment or gave our heroine a makeover amidst a volley of humorous quips, and then exited stage right in time for her to have hot sex with the het hero.

While this was definitely a step up from the serial killer of years past, the vast majority of the time that they appeared, those stereotypical gay characters were neutered and usually asexual. They were gay in appearance and attitude, but any potential hot man-on-man action was carefully left out. It was, for the most part, at least in the world of mainstream romance novels, not even mentioned.

Shhhh.

Where were the gay people that I knew? The regular people who lived down the street from me? The kind for whom being gay meant falling in love with someone of the same gender, and then having steamy, romance-novel-worthy sex?

I wasn't finding them in what I was reading, so I decided to include those characters in my own stories.

In 1999 (back when Jason was thirteen), I started writing my Troubleshooters series of romantic suspense novels for Ballantine Books. I was pretty sure this new series that featured a team of Navy SEALs was going to be well-received and widely popular, at least judging from the success of the books I'd written up to this point in my career.

I was also highly aware, *because* I'd been writing military-themed romantic suspense for quite a few years, that my readership was largely conservative, both politically and socially. I knew I had a chance, through my books, to stretch the boundaries and the comfort zones of at least *some* of those readers.

And I decided to introduce an openly out gay FBI agent named Jules Cassidy as a major secondary character in this ongoing series. My plan was to have Jules's character return in book after book after book, and challenge some of those readers' preconceived notions and beliefs about what it meant to be gay.

I approached this idea very carefully, planning out Jules's journey in advance. I'm an outliner when it comes to writing, and I often plot five- or six-book story arcs well in advance. So doing this was not difficult for me.

But here's what I did:

In Troubleshooters book #2, *The Defiant Hero*, I introduce Jules Cassidy as the FBI partner of Alyssa Locke, one of my most important female characters, a character with an on-going story arc of her own. I let Jules be the kind of gay character that my readers would recognize and accept: the witty sidekick. He's funny and smart, but he's also a highly skilled and extremely kickass FBI agent. I make it very clear that Alyssa trusts him with her life.

Alyssa also has a romantic interest in the series—a very testosterone-driven Navy SEAL from Texas, named Sam Starrett. Sam's vaguely homophobic ignorance creates a conflict from the moment that he and Jules meet. In fact, Sam's personal journey throughout the series was designed to be intentionally parallel (or I hoped it would be!) to that of my conservative readers'. He would voice their concerns, and be there to hold their hands as I urged them to step outside of their comfort zone.

In the next book, TS #3, *Over the Edge*, Jules and Sam and Alyssa are back. Jules again proves himself to be a highly skilled FBI agent. By working closely with Jules, Sam begins to get to know and trust him, and the two men begin a tentative friendship. Sam's ignorance (and homophobia) is being erased as he sees Jules as a person and not just "one of those scary and different gay guys."

In this book, again, Jules is not just a witty sidekick, he's a full-on, kickass action hero who just happens to be gay.

In TS #4, *Out of Control*, Jules is back, interacting with a variety of new characters. He is the FBI agent (read: action hero) who has the answers and the skill to save the day. Again and again, I hammer home to my readers the fact that Jules is worthy of their respect and affection.

Also, this book is when I first mention that Jules has a boyfriend named Adam. Who lives with him. As in, they share an apartment and, yes, a bed. But I keep their relationship off the page. We don't see Adam, but Jules talks about him the way that all people talk about their significant others. Adam exists, and the reader (and Sam) learns that Jules has an active and satisfying sex life with a partner whom he loves.

This is a step beyond witty sidekick/action hero. Jules is no longer asexual, even though the conservative readers are a safe distance from the hot m/m action.

Still, the world didn't end.

In fact, the series was becoming more and more popular with each and every book. And when I went out on book tours, even in deeply red states like Oklahoma, the very first question I got when holding Q&A sessions was always, "Will we be seeing more of Jules Cassidy?"

I remember a booksigning in the deep south where I received a standing ovation, merely at the mention of Jules's name.

This character was, without a doubt, a solid reader favorite.

In TS #5, *Into the Night*, Sam finds out that Adam has left Jules, and that Jules is heartbroken. And, learning that, Sam is allowed to grow even more in his acceptance of Jules. Sam (and my readers) see Jules as a person who loves, and who hurts upon loss of that love—just like any other person on this planet. Love is love.

More books followed, and whenever I needed an FBI agent to save the day, I brought Jules into the series. By doing this, I hammered home to my readers that he was a kickass, patriotic, highly skilled hero who was worthy of winning his own happily ever after.

Now here's where the message got a little conflicted for my conservative readers.

In book after book, they had come to know Jules as a friend, and like Sam, their ignorance-based homophobia had faded. They saw that Jules was a hero, that he was smart and funny and strong. That he was worthy and honorable and true.

But what does the traditional hero of a romance novel win at the end of a book?

He wins his HEA ending.

"And they lived happily ever after."

To my more conservative readership, an HEA ending includes commitment through marriage.

And there was my question to them: *Why shouldn't Jules deserve the exact same HEA ending as any other romance hero? Didn't Jules deserve to marry the man of his dreams?*

At the same time, I was pushing the envelope even farther in terms of my inclusion of LGBT characters in mainstream romance novels.

In TS # 8, *Hot Target*, I finally—*finally*!—included a major romantic subplot for Jules. In this book, Jules meets a young Hollywood actor named Robin Chadwick. And sparks fly.

But I took it slowly, not wanting to frighten off my conservative readers. I wanted readers who had never read m/m before (and who probably had no idea that such a genre even existed!) to focus on the similar, on these two characters' emotional connection, rather than on the differences between f/m and m/m sex.

Still, in the course of this book, Jules and Robin share several rather steamy kisses as they deal with the intense emotions they both feel.

When this mainstream romance novel with a gay romantic subplot was published, the sky didn't fall. In fact, *Hot Target* hit the Times list particularly hard, and even won an award for the Borders Group's best selling hardcover romance of the year.

But I still had more work to do, because Jules's romantic story arc was far from over.

And in TS #11, *Force of Nature*, Jules and Robin return, and they win their happy ending.

Again, because I was bringing a same sex relationship into a mainstream romance novel, I made the difficult choice to pull some amount of gauze over the virtual camera lens when the two men became intimate. As I wrote in a blog that I wrote and posted on my website after that book was released,

> "I have to admit that I'm bracing for some
> complaints from (my more progressive)
> readers -- the first having to do with the
> non-graphic nature of the Jules/Robin love

scene.

> I really struggled with the best way to write
> this scene, because to me it does seem
> unbalanced—to have the [heterosexual
> couple's] love scenes be so graphic, but
> then to leave so much to the imagination in
> the limo with Robin and Jules."

But my message—love is love is love—is so important, I just couldn't bear the thought of frightening away a more timid readership by putting in too much man-on-man action. And I believe that the truth is—at least *my* truth — that making love is about emotions. I felt the most important part of the Robin/Jules love scene was how Jules felt when Robin confessed that he *loved* him.

And oh, wasn't that a lovely problem to have? To worry that my more progressive readers would be disappointed that the m/m sex wasn't graphic enough?

Still, throughout the writing of this story arc, it was not my intention to "preach to the choir." My intention was to hang on to as many conservative, traditional romance readers as possible, in an attempt to change the way they viewed the world.

It was shortly after writing *Force of Nature* that I came up with the idea for *All Through the Night*, TS #12, the book in which Jules and Robin get married in Boston.

There was also a pressing civil rights reason why I wrote ATTN. I'd been fighting for equal marriage in Massachusetts for years, supporting a kickass LGBT rights group called MassEquality. I got a mayday call from their head organizers when a battle we'd thought we'd won came roaring back to life, like some bad imitation of Frankenstein's monster.

We were exhausted and bitterly disappointed.

I'd done my share of phone-banking and canvassing through the years, and I not only hated it, but I also sucked at it.

But writing? *That* I could do. I decided to write the story of

Jules's and Robin's wedding, and to give all of my earnings for this book--advances, subrights, and royalties into perpetuity—to MassEquality.

The money was used effectively, the battle was won, and the book, which was the first-ever mainstream romance novel with a hero and a hero, hit the New York Times hardcover fiction list.

I've brought Jules (and Robin) back in just about all of the Troubleshooter novels and e-short-stories I've written since then. Jules continues to be a kickass FBI agent, and to help save the day. Robin continues to love him madly.

All throughout my Troubleshooters series, my message was this:

Meet Jules. Jules is worthy. He is a highly skilled, heroic FBI agent who happens to be gay.

Love is love is love—and all love should be celebrated.

Having Jules on the team isn't unusual or strange in any way. His being gay is not a big deal to the Navy SEALs and to the FBI agents who work with him.

Being gay is *normal*.

And that's what I mean by *redefining normal*.

When we have a gay friend or family member, we realize that being gay is no big thing. It's just one small part of who our friend or family member is. We learn through experience that being gay is no different than being right-handed or having freckles or being tall.

And the more gay family members and friends (and fictional friends count!) that we encounter, the more we come to recognize that normal includes families with gay children or fathers or mothers or sisters, cousins, aunts. Normal is attending school with gay teachers and gay students. Normal is going to church and worshipping with gay clergy and congregation members.

Normal is living in an America in which gay citizens enjoy the exact same civil rights as every other American.

As a writer, I have control. As a writer, I design the specs for my fictional universe. I work hard to establish and to build a realistic world in which my books are set, a world in which my characters live and breathe and connect with one another.

And my world is one where kids can grow up believing—correctly—that being gay is an option and suicide is *not*.

Life, as they say, imitates art.

I've received thousands of emails from readers for whom Jules was their very first out gay friend—readers whose hearts and minds were radically changed from meeting Jules; readers who now staunchly believe that Jules—and Jason—should be able to marry the person he loves, whether he lives in Massachusetts or California or North Carolina.

And while I know that I probably can't change the fear-and-ignorance-driven thinking of people like that woman who held that awful sign and said such viciously hateful things to Jason all those years ago, my outrage and sorrow is made bearable by knowing that there's an army of "friends of Jules" out there who now fully recognize that that woman and her fellow Kool aid-drinkers are pathetic, small-minded, and woefully misguided.

And a soon to be thing-of-the-past.

Suck it. Bitch.

◆　　◆　　◆

CHAPTER ONE
REPORTING FOR DUTY

We've discussed marriage, children, religion, politics, discrimination, family feuds, falling-outs, falling in love, acceptance, equality, true love, and sex in the bedroom—in fact, pretty much everything you're *not* supposed to discuss in polite society. But hey, that's just the kinda guy I am.

As you read this book you'll notice that Kris, while editing and laying out the project, chose different fonts to help you identify each person's involvement in Gay Romance, i.e., whether someone is a reader, author, reviewer, cover artist, editor, or publisher. It should help you keep track of the interviewees and why they answer some questions from a certain angle. I should mention that some of the interviewees are involved in Gay Romance on several levels; in those cases we tried to choose the role that best defines them.

You'll also notice that once in a while I'll jump in with a different question. I tried to keep this to a minimum because I wanted these women to be the voice of this book... but every now and then something came up and I just had to know more!

But enough from me. Now it's time to introduce you to the women who made this book possible; where they live, how old they are, what their household situation is, how I met them, and why I wanted their involvement in this project. These women have amazed, inspired, surprised, amused, but most of all enlightened me! I love each and every one of them, and I think you will too. So here they are:

◆　　◆　　◆

ALLY (Author of Gay Romance)

Name: Ally Blue

Relationship/Household Status: Married with Children (but not like the TV show because my hubby and kids are AWESOME)

Age Group: I was twelve when my country (the U.S.A.) celebrated its bicentennial. If you really want to know how old I am, do the math, it's good for your brain :D (mom moment)

Lives in: One of those wide places in the road somewhere outside Asheville, North Carolina, USA

Should Frodo and Sam be more than just best friends? What do the Harry Potter novels have to do with straight women loving Gay Romance? These are the secrets Ally Blue revealed as we talked about everything from fan fiction to family matters. Ally is one of those extraordinary women who has managed to raise children, work in a profession that saves lives, and still manage to find the time to write novels… a lot of them! She is passionate, funny, clever, and one of Gay Romance's most prolific authors.

◆   ◆   ◆

AMELIA (Writer for the Huffington Post)

Name: Amelia

Relationship/Household Status: Married with Children Plus One

Age Group: Too old to be wearing miniskirts, but young enough not to lie about my age (30s)

Lives in: Midwest, USA

One of the true revelations that emerged while working on this project was the importance of family. When we approached Suzanne Brockmann to write a piece for this book, one of the first things Suz did was ask if her friend Amelia could be involved as well. Amelia is a writer for the Huffington Post website and when I discovered her unique family situation, I simply knew she had to be a part of this project.

◆ ◆ ◆

AMY (Reader of Gay Romance)

Name: Amy

Relationship/Household Status: I recently went on a date with a man who plucked his nose hair in front of me so the answer is a resounding Single and Fabulous!

Age Group: I actually used to listen to New Kids on the Block *hangs head in shame!*

Lives in: Ormond Beach, Florida, USA

I first met Amy at GayRomLit in New Orleans 2011. We may have been involved in some group discussions online in the lead-up to GRL, but there's nothing quite like meeting Amy in person! She has a big voice and an even bigger heart, which is probably the combined result of her Italian-American background and the fact that she was pretty much raised in a household full of boys. She's loyal, loving, will smack you down if you're out of line… then give you a big hug! Amy is also one of the founders of the MANtastic bookclub dedicated to Gay Romance or M/M Fiction.

◆ ◆ ◆

ANKE (Reader of Gay Romance)

Name: Anke

Relationship/Household Status: Married with Children (but not like the TV show)

Age Group: Happy to be where I'm now, although it prompted the question from my youngest, whether we already had TV when I was young?!? He was quite astonished to learn that in fact we had TV, but only 3 channels and no program during the day.

Lives in: Southern Germany

I wanted Anke for this project because she lives in Germany

and I wanted to know more about her world and where Gay Romance fits with German society. When Anke told me she wasn't sure if she was the right person because nobody really knew about her love for Gay Romance apart from other readers and authors, I really wanted her for the project! Anke is a kind, gentle, and intelligent woman with three grown children, and a loving husband with whom she travels the globe (when I first asked her to be a part of this book, her reply came from Kenya). As a traveller, Anke has a passion for exploring new places and discovering new things. I think it's fair to say she now counts Gay Romance as one of her favorite journeys.

◆   ◆   ◆

ANNE (Author of Gay Romance)

Name: Anne Brooke, Author

Relationship/Household Status: Married and Happily Without Children

Age Group: 47 and proud of it. Anyway, who needs a group?...

Lives in: Elstead, near Guildford, Surrey, UK

Anne and I first met through a mutual publisher and her writing instantly grabbed my attention. Her work is beautiful and accessible. Long or short, playful or poetic, Anne's choice of words is always careful and considered yet her writing is so courageous. But the woman herself is even more so! I confess I truly adore this intelligent, articulate, bold Christian woman living in the English countryside and writing some of the best Gay Romance and Gay Erotica on the planet.

◆   ◆   ◆

CAROL (Author of Gay Romance)

Name: Carol Lynne

Relationship/Household Status: Divorced with Kids (I Am Woman, Hear Me Roar!)

Age Group: Let me put it this way, I used to watch the original

Charlie's Angels in primetime, along with The Waltons and Little House on the Prairie. I'm sure some of you thought those old shows have always been shown on obscure cable channels during the middle of the day, but once upon a time, they were on major television networks.

Lives in: Kansas City, USA

For the record, Carol Lynne is an amazing woman on so many levels. When I first met Carol I felt an instant connection with her. She is smart, funny, and no bullshit... my kinda person, plus she had already earned my admiration as an organizer of GayRomLit and one of the most prolific and respected authors in Gay Romance. But during this project I got to know Carol so much more. If anybody reading this book right now needs to transform their life, rise from the ashes, and discover their true calling, Carol is your inspiration. Carol continues to inspire and challenge me, and I consider myself fortunate that I can call her my friend.

◆　◆　◆

DAWN (Reviewer of Gay Romance)

Name: Dawn Roberto who also writes as Raine Delight

Relationship/Household Status: Single with Kids (I Am Woman, Hear Me Roar!) with a SO of six years

Age Group: *smiles* Mid-30's and in the prime of my life

Lives in: Small town in Western New York, USA, about 40 minutes from Buffalo and Rochester

Dawn is something of a unique creature, which is why I wanted her for this project. Not only is she a voracious reader of Gay Romance, she's also an author as well as being a reviewer, blogger, and running one of the most popular Yahoo groups on Gay Romance. Dawn is a force to be reckoned with in terms of her online presence, and since the internet is arguably the birthplace of Gay Romance, I needed to talk to an expert like Dawn on the power of the internet and how the worldwide web became the foundation of an entire category of romance and its legions of fans.

◆   ◆   ◆

DOLORIANNE (Reader of Gay Romance)

Name: Dolorianne

Relationship/Household Status: Single

Age Group: In high school my favorite bands were Heart, Extreme, Foreigner, Europe, Bon Jovi, Poison, Skid Row... yes I loved most "hair" bands!

Lives in: Ormond Beach, Florida, United States

Who'd have thought a bookclub that came into being as a result of a Twilight obsession would lead to one of the biggest Gay Romance bookclubs in America, but when Dolorianne's sister started her club full of Twi-hard fans, Dolorianne met Amy and introduced her to Gay Romance books, forming a sub-club of the bookclub. From there, Sheri and eventually Eugenia Lynn joined them. After Amy suggested I ask Dolorianne to be involved in this project, Dolorianne sent me the most passionate and articulate email detailing her views on attitudes and perceptions of homosexuality from the 1950s to today. Needless to say, I recruited her straight away! Dolorianne is sweet, smart, and extremely savvy, and is the founder of what is now the online bookclub and M/M fiction resource site http://mantasticfiction.wordpress.com which she maintains daily with the help of the other MANtastic gals!

◆   ◆   ◆

ELISA (Reviewer of Gay Romance)

Name: Elisa

Relationship/Household Status: Single and Fabulous and always in motion

Age Group: my first crush was Patrick Swayze in Dirty Dancing ;-)

Lives in: Italy

Elisa is truly the principessa of Gay Romance. Her website — elisa-rolle.livejournal.com — is one of the most comprehensive online journals dedicated solely to gay literature, art, and film ever created. A successful, multi-lingual career woman in her own right, Elisa's job takes her all around the world, yet not only does she somehow manage to still find the time to review books, run competitions, write articles and interview authors for her site, in the last few years Elisa also launched the Rainbow Awards, an online annual awards event that judges hundreds of gay titles in dozens of categories. Elisa is also one of the sweetest people I've ever met, and when I found out why she loves gay romance so much, her reason was just as sweet as she is! Keep reading and you'll see what I mean.

◆   ◆   ◆

EMILY (Reader of Gay Romance)

Name: Emily

Relationship/Household Status: Single and Fabulous

Age Group: The year I graduated high school the movie Shrek, hit the big screen.

Lives in: QLD, Australia

I have met several mothers and daughters who love Gay Romance and this was something I really wanted to include in the book. One such mother/daughter pairing is Norma (mum) and Emily (daughter), two wonderful, down-to-earth, tell-it-like-it-is Australian women from the Queensland countryside whose introduction to Gay Romance is one of the most touching stories in this book. And while Emily's responses may well be the shortest in the book, I totally adore the confident, young, no-apologies attitude in almost every answer she gives.

◆   ◆   ◆

ERICA (Author of Gay Romance)

Name: Erica Pike

Relationship/Household Status: Single mother of twins (to those who want twins, you don't know what you're asking for!)

Age Group: I did the "Running Man" to "2 Unlimited" as a teen – look it up if either of those look unfamiliar.

Lives in: Iceland, Europe

Iceland! I knew nothing about Iceland until I met Erica, an amazing, funny, energetic, proudly-spoken yet quietly-introverted woman from a nation with a total population of just over 300,000! How much did I want Erica in this book! We had met online, which is pretty much the only connection Erica has to the world of Gay Romance, so interviewing her gave me the opportunity to explore her life, her world, her community so much more. Erica's interview is one of my favorites because I learned so much... about the country, the culture, and the woman. Thanks, Erica!

◆   ◆   ◆

HELEN (Author of Gay Romance)

Name: Helen

Relationship/Household Status: Married empty nester with too much time on her hands.

Age Group: Let's just say the first concert I attended was The Monkees when I was in high school.

Lives in: Sydney, Australia

It's fair to say you wouldn't be reading this book right now if not for Helen. When I first considered pitching this project to Laura and Kris, I first asked Helen whether I should or not. Her simple response was "Do it!". Helen is instrumental in my writing in every way (advice, ideas, inspiration, proofing, editing, whip-cracking!). She was the first female fan of mine I ever met, and now, heck, she's practically my manager. But more than that, Helen's one of the best friends I've ever had. There was no possible way I could write this book without including her. Thanks buddy!

◆   ◆   ◆

J. ROSE (Author and Editor of Gay Romance)

Name: J. Rose Allister

Relationship/Household Status: Married (but not dead), Mother, Grandmother—and too young to be one!

Age Group: Old enough to know better and too young to care

Lives in: Southern California, USA

I wanted J. Rose to be a part of this project because she has played such an important part in my introduction to Gay Romance…and as it turned out, during our interview I discovered that I had unwittingly done the same for her. When I first started out writing Gay Romance and Gay Erotica, J. Rose was an Acquisitions Editor who picked up my work. I didn't know until I asked her to be a part of this project that I was her first encounter with Gay Erotica. She loved my manuscript and I loved working with her, and we instantly clicked. J. Rose is one of those beautiful souls, open-minded in every respect and a true writing talent in her own right!

◆   ◆   ◆

JEN (Author of Gay Romance)

Name: Jen

Relationship/Household Status: Married with Child

Age Group: End of the Baby Boomers

Lives in: Massachusetts, USA

At GRL in New Orleans I got to know Jen quite well and I even had the honor of meeting her gorgeous daughter (attending college in New Orleans) who doesn't read Gay Romance herself but over lunch it was obvious to me that she completely respects her mother and has a live-and-let-live attitude towards Jen's passion for Gay Romance. I adore Jen, she's a life-lover and the perfect example of someone whose life has changed as a result of Gay Romance. Jen went from not knowing any gay men at all, to seeking them out, making friends, joining groups and is now one of the most pro-active supporters of gay rights I know, simply because she believes everyone should have their Happily Ever After.

◆   ◆   ◆

JET (Author of Gay Romance)

Name: Jet Mykles (pseudonym)

Relationship/Household Status: In a domestic partnership with my boyfriend for 14 yrs.

Age Group: I remember a time before microwaves. I also remember black and white televisions with a knob when remote controls were a fancy new gadget that rarely anyone had. We got our first "PC" back before people even really knew what that was and we were jazzed that it had dual floppy drives (no hard drive).

Lives in: Los Angeles County, California

I loved interviewing Jet so much, mainly because I could see the story of Jet come through in her answers. I don't mean the stories she tells, I'm referring to the story of Jet's life, her world, the transitions in her journey that Gay Romance has made possible. And I love that Jet's not the only one; this is a book about personal stories and individual journeys. As Jet summed up in one of her answers, "Writing erotic romance has helped me because I care less about what other people think of me… It's very freeing." Jet means this not just in a good way, but in the best way possible. If more of us did the things that open the cage door and give us wings—rather than doing the things that others expect us to do—I dare say the world would be a truly wonderful place.

◆   ◆   ◆

KIMBER (Author of Gay Romance)

Name: Kimberly Gardner

Relationship/Household Status: I've been married for twenty years, no biological children but I do have one stepdaughter. Nothing very drama-worthy I'd say.

Age Group: About to turn 27 for the 22nd time

Lives in: Pennsylvania (though not in the scary middle)

I had never really spoken to Kimber before this project, but this wonderful author pounced on this project with so much gusto and enthusiasm that it made me so grateful to have her on board. For me, Kimber truly represents that person out there who discovers the joys of reading Gay Romance and loves it so much that they become one of its shining lights. As Kimber points out, it's easy for non-fans of traditional romance to judge it as "the maligned step-child of genre fiction." So what does that make Gay Romance?! Is the book world ready for a shake-up?

◆ ◆ ◆

KRIS (Editor of Gay Romance)

Name: Kris Jacen

Relationship/Household Status: Married with Children (but not like the TV show)

Age Group: I'm a child of the 80s…bring on some Duran Duran!

Lives in: Western New York, USA

Kris! My words, my life, my editor… for every good writer knows that writing is for writers, editing is for editors! Hand over those babies and let your editor do their job (rather than listen to you bitch and moan)… that's a lesson for any writer to learn quickly. And Kris is one of the best. But she's more than an editor to me; she's a friend, advisor, confidante, and sounding board. So naturally Kris had to be a part of this book, not just for the thankless, all-important job of editing, but as one of my interviewees. Devoted wife, mother, career woman, and editor, my hat is off to you Kris… none of us would be reading this right now if not for you!

◆   ◆   ◆

LAURA (Publisher and Author of Gay Romance)

Name: Laura Baumbach

Relationship/Household Status: My husband and I will celebrate our 31st Wedding Anniversary this holiday season. We were married the day after Christmas. He said it was the perfect day so he could remember it. In truth, he had accepted a job in CA with General Dynamics and we had to leave PA after the New Year. I refused to move across the country with him without being married. Just engaged wasn't cutting it. This girl's no free ride. <g> Nine years later we adopted our first son. Eight years after that, our second. So I guess that makes me Married with Other People's Children!

Age Group: Well, Donna Summers was my favorite singer to dance to, if that gives you a clue. I love the BeeGees, the Monkees, and Dolly Parton. Yes, I have always been…eclectic.

Lives in: Presently I am feeling stranded in a small agricultural town in western New York State, USA. It was great to raise the kids in my 30's and 40's, but now I'm wanting to be closer to the action again. Plays, concerts, art festivals-- I feel the need to get out and be part of life on a different level at this age. Warm weather year round wouldn't hurt. <g>

I truly believe that Laura is a cornerstone of the M/M industry. I didn't simply want Laura to be the person to publish this book; I needed her. I needed her drive and her knowledge and her guidance, without which I could not have pulled this project together. Laura has been a pioneer and crusader for Gay Romance longer than most of us have been reading or writing it, which is why I wanted her to have the final say at the end of this book. Her story is one of determination, survival, and true belief in one's dreams.

◆   ◆   ◆

LYNN (Reader of Gay Romance)

Name: Eugenia Lynn

Relationship/Household Status: I'm Married with one child

Age Group: Duran Duran was my favorite band in High School

Lives in: Palm Coast, Florida

Eugenia Lynn was the fourth to join the MANtastic bookclub and there were questions as to whether Lynn would actually enjoy or even want to read about Gay Romance. Why? Because Lynn has a gay son. Would reading Gay Romance spill his sexual secrets, or even worse, in her mind would Lynn be unable to separate her son's life from what was on the page? Once again, here was another intriguing perspective to explore, another compelling story to tell, another uncharted trail to tread, that made Lynn's involvement in this project a must. Oh, and did I mention that she's also a fabulous person?

◆   ◆   ◆

NORMA (Author of Gay Romance)

Name: Norma

Relationship/Household Status: Married with Children (but not like the TV show)

Age Group: When I was a teen my bedroom walls were covered in Brian Mannix (Uncanny Xmen) and Boy George posters.

Lives in: QLD, Australia.

As I mentioned in Emily's intro, one of the biggest reasons I wanted Norma and Emily as part of this project was to discuss the topic of mothers and daughters both reading Gay Romance and sharing their love for these books. But something even more interesting in this relationship is Norma not only reads M/M fiction, she writes some of the most beautiful Gay Romance novels on the market. Of course, neither women was allowed to discuss their answers to my questions with each other—in fact, that was the same rule for every participant in the book; no interviewee read anyone else's responses until the project was complete—so let's bring Norma and Emily out of their booths of silence and compare answers, shall we!

◆ ◆ ◆

PETCHIE (Reader of Gay Romance)

Name: Perpetua

Relationship/Household Status: Married with Children (but not like the TV show....well okay maybe a little like the show!)

Age Group: Okay so I have no idea what to put in here it's a lot easier to be smart and sarcastic when you're not thinking about it! So I just turned 33 this June maybe we can come up with something later?

Lives in: Northern Ireland

Petchie has been an online friend for several years and I adore her. She's a bold Irish lass with a caring soul and a wicked sense of humor. In fact, the only thing missing when you talk to Petchie online is a pint of Guinness and a steaming pot of Irish stew…which is why I wanted her involved in this project; to discuss how living in Ireland and the geographic distance from so many others in the Gay Romance community impacts her on a personal level. Can oceans hold someone back from being one of the biggest fans of Gay Romance on the planet? Given she was born with the name Perpetua, I have no doubt that Petchie will 'perpetually' do everything she can to keep her love affair with Gay Romance thriving, no matter the distance.

◆ ◆ ◆

P.L. (Cover Artist for Gay Romance)

Name: P.L. Nunn

Relationship/Household Status: Single and Fabulous

Age Group: Old enough to know better, young enough to still

get into trouble.

Lives in: Virginia, USA

When I began workshopping this project with MLR Press, Laura reminded me to not only invite readers and authors to participate, but also someone who does the cover art for Gay Romance. And so we asked P.L. Nunn, one of the best cover artists in the industry, to join our book to discuss Gay Romance on a visual level. Do we really judge books by their covers? How does someone take words on a page and turn them into the image that will sell a Gay Romance? What are straight women looking for, chiselled torsos…or tender kisses?

◆   ◆   ◆

POPPY (Author of Gay Romance)

Name: Poppy

Relationship/Household Status: Messy

Age Group: Remembers when Madonna was Like a Virgin

Lives in: Southeast United States

My writer's love affair with Poppy began when she asked me to write an episode of Boxer Falls, a free gaytime soap opera which has a different writer of Gay Romance adding a new episode every week online, with the goal to print the complete anthologized volume of Season One at the end of the year with all profits being donated to GLAAD (Gay & Lesbian Alliance Against Defamation). As a result I've made an amazing new friend whose recently-published first Gay Romance novel Mind Magic was an instant bestseller! Poppy is the sweetest, shyest, loveliest creature I've ever met, with a great big heart and now it would seem a great big talent to match. A Pop-star is born!

◆   ◆   ◆

RO (Reader of Gay Romance)

Name: Rosemary aka Ro

Relationship/Household Status: Divorced, after twenty years I discovered I really did not like him. Empty nester, two daughters grown and gone (peace at last)

Age Group: I was born when Harry S. Truman was President and a "party line" was a shared telephone system.

Lives in: Kansas City, Missouri, USA

The one thing I knew about Ro when I asked her to be a part of this project was the woman had an energy, a spark, a tell-it-like-it-is voice that I wanted in this book! If you want polite lies, you don't go to Ro. If you want politically correct puffery when the damn straight facts will do just fine, you don't go to Ro. What you do go to Ro for is honesty, heart, and a healthy helping of kick-ass attitude! I love her! When it comes to Gay Romance, Ro is one helluva straight talker!

◆　◆　◆

SHERI (Reader of Gay Romance)

Name: Sheri

Relationship/Household Status: Married with Children (but not like the TV show). Ok, maybe a little like the show minus the big hair, and the sex-deprived wife. My husband attacks me every chance he gets and I like it like that.

Age Group: Old as dirt, as my kid would say, little brats. Madonna was still a virgin and Elton John was straight, when I was young. I'm 40ish and still loving life.

Lives in: Ormond Beach, Florida, USA

The lovely Sher-Bear was the third woman to join the MANtastic gals, swapping Twilight for books where men take their shirts off for each other, not Bella. But it's all the elements of Gay Romance that Sheri loves, from the action in the bedroom to the sweet kisses and Happily Ever Afters. Speaking of bedrooms, after my interview with Sheri I seriously want to meet her husband! You'll find out why a little later.

◆ ◆ ◆

STEPHANI (Author of Gay Romance)

Name: Stephani Hecht

Relationship/Household Status: Married with two bratty, yet wonderful kids

Age Group: Old enough to know the names of all the Brady kids, but young enough to have never owned an 8-track

Lives in: Holly, Michigan, USA

This book was one of those projects that could have gone on forever (and I hope the discussion indeed does). There were so many more women I wanted in this book but if I had kept inviting people to participate, the book never would have been published. Yet at the 11th hour, with my deadline looming, I just had to ask Stephani Hecht to be involved, firstly because she's a wonderful and prolific writer of gay romance, secondly because she backs up her writing by being a hands-on equal rights activist in the GLBTQ community, and thirdly because her gay son Cody has now become a prominent voice for gay youth and equal rights. Stephani's story in the final chapter sums up all the reasons I wanted to do this project in the first place.

◆ ◆ ◆

SUZ (New York Times Bestselling Romance Author) Name: Suzanne Brockmann

Relationship/Household Status: Married (for 29 years!) with two grown children

Age Group: Born in 1960 -- I am proudly at the start of my second half-century!

Lives in: Siesta Key, Florida, USA (a short bike ride to the beach)

Well you've all met Suz already: proud Mom of a talented gay son, New York Times No. 1 Bestselling Author, and writer of the best ever last line in an essay! My publisher Laura was the one who wanted Suzanne Brockmann for this project. Laura emailed Suz and without a moment's hesitation Suz was on board. Not only was she a sheer pleasure to work with on this project; she was inspiring, kind, knowing and wise, completely down-to-earth, and so incredibly generous with her time despite her many commitments and busy writing schedule. But what I loved about working with Suz the most was… she got it! From that very first email, Suz instantly understood everything Laura, Kris, and I wanted to achieve with this project and saw the value and potential and power of this book… then hit every nail on the head bang-on with every word she typed. I will be eternally grateful to her, and to Jason too (thanks for being you, mister! The world is now a better place simply because your Mom loves you so much!)

◆   ◆   ◆

TERESA (Reader of Gay Romance)

Name: Teresa

Relationship/Household Status: Single Empty Nester (Loving Life Now)

Age Group: 46

Lives in: Needles, California

When I first met Teresa at GayRomLit in New Orleans, she walked straight up to me and said, "My Mom loves your books." It was one of the pivotal moments that made me want to do this project. Instantly I wanted to know more: why did Teresa lend her Mom my books, did they discuss them in detail, why do straight women—mothers and daughters—love Gay Romance? Over the next few days, I spent a lot of time with Teresa to discover she is one of the loveliest, most genuine people I've ever met. She is also a true devotee of Gay Romance and reads everything the minute it's released. When I asked her to be part of this project she told me she was worried her answers would be boring. My response was, "None of you are boring. The world is going to find you fascinating. Just be yourself!"

◆ ◆ ◆

TRACY (Reader of Gay Romance)

Name: Tracy

Relationship/Household Status: Single and Fabulous

Age Group: I was down with OPP

Lives in: Philadelphia, PA, USA

Tracy loves Disneyland, the happiest place on the planet, so it's no wonder that Tracy is very possibly the happiest person on Earth! Tracy is a bubble of fun ready to burst open with positive energy and overwhelming enthusiasm and generosity, complete with an infectious laugh and always-beaming face. But after asking Tracy to take part in this project, she added the term "full of surprises" to my perception of her, as the fun-loving girl I met in New Orleans blossomed into the complex creature she truly is—intelligent, certain of herself yet not without humility, and yes, constantly brimming with positive energy as I'm sure she always will be.

◆ ◆ ◆

VERITARABBIT (Reader of Gay Romance)

Name: Veritarabbit

Relationship/Household Status: Married with a daughter

Age Group: 30's, old enough to remember Back Street Boys when they were actually boys

Lives in: Hong Kong

I met Veritarabbit online after she read my first gay novel, *The Cross of Sins*, and told me how much she loved my characters; she even sent me her thoughts on who she'd cast in a film version of the book, which is an incredible compliment for an author; it means your words have truly come to life for the reader. Veritarabbit is South Korean but considers Hong Kong her home, so I knew she would bring an amazing cultural diversity to this project. I wanted to show that the straight female fanbase of Gay Romance was not simply limited to the United States or even the western world; it is a global phenomenon and Veritarabbit's insightful and intelligent interview helps demonstrate that. Thank you, my friend!

◆　◆　◆

WAVE (Reviewer of Gay Romance)

Name: Wave

Age Group: Here's the dirt. I'll never see thirty again. Who the hell am I kidding? I'll never see forty again. Maybe I can tweak the age thing a little higher after a few drinks, but only if you're buying. My age is consistent with the music I listen to but I'm only going to confuse you by saying that I love those old geezers the Rolling Stones, Elton John and Bruce Springsteen but I also rock Mary J. Blige, the Dixie Chicks, Whitney Houston, Journey, Prince, Bon Jovi, Lady Gaga and a mixed bag of singers who are all on my iPod. Now you're totally confused aren't you? That was my intention

Lives in: Toronto, Canada

The thing I love about Wave is that she lives up to her name... she makes waves! But let's face it, getting noticed is exactly what Gay Romance needs, and waving that rainbow flag is something Wave does exceptionally well. Her website is dedicated to M/M fiction, packed with news, reviews, interviews, and giveaways, and is one of the major online destinations in the world for all things Gay Romance. But be warned, Wave tells it like it is. She opts for critique over compliments, gives praise only where it's due, and demands quality on every level in the books she reads. And why should anybody settle for less?

◆　◆　◆

Z (Author of Gay Romance)

Name: Z. Allora

Relationship/Household Status: Love Slave for almost 20 happy years

Age Group: When I was in high school rock stars understood hair and make-up was important.

Lived in: The last five and half years I was living in Suzhou, China but I grew up in a small town in Upstate NY. I spent a year in Singapore, two-years living in Israel, and lived in CA, AZ, and PA. I am now back in the good ole US of A but I still consider myself a New Yorker even though the state I live in has 'south' in the name of it. (Over the past twenty-two years, I have moved thirteen times and I have traveled to twenty-nine different countries).

I wanted Z on this project for a number of reasons: not only is she a great writer of Gay Romance, but this American author lived for several years in mainland China, which differs greatly from Hong Kong. As Veritarabbit points out, Hong Kong is and also has been relatively open-minded, but by comparison, Z's experiences of mainland China portray a country and culture capable of oppression and discrimination, where an industry like Gay Romance is difficult to access and virtually impossible to discuss. Her interview is truly eye-opening and made me want to march even faster—and wave our flag even higher—on our journey towards equal rights. And in the process I discovered a woman who is exciting, funny, complex, and clever! Thanks for sharing, Z!

◆ ◆ ◆

CHAPTER TWO
UNCHARTED TERRITORY

If this category of romance is such a secret, how did these women find out about it? That was the first thing I wanted to ask when I started these interviews. Were they introduced to it by a friend or did they just stumble upon it? Did they enter into their first book cautiously or did they tear open the cover and devour it whole? What went through their minds as they delved into a world of hot sex and passionate kisses between two men? Had they stepped into a secret forbidden world...or did they feel like they were coming home to a place they belonged? And what exactly was it that made them want more?

◆　　◆　　◆

Kimber

I've been a romance reader since adolescence, cutting my teeth on those old Harlequin novels that appeared in abridged form in the pages of *Good Housekeeping* magazine (now I am seriously dating myself). Lol!

About six years ago I had become very bored with traditional romance to the point that even the growing erotic romance genre seemed to have little new to offer me as a reader. It's important to note here that I've been an eBook fan for many years and I have eagerly shopped the ebook publishers because they are so often on the cutting edge of what is new and exciting in genre fiction. That's how I discovered my very first gay romance novel. It was J.L. Langley's *The Tin Star*.

I remember thinking "Wow! This is incredibly hot!" But it was so much more than the hotness factor of seeing two sexy men together. Because I love romance, the act of falling in love, it was that process which most captivated me.

◆　　◆　　◆

Dolorianne

When I started reading M/M it was because JR Ward's BDB (Black Dagger Brotherhood) series was hinting at a M/M pairing. That was more than 4 years and 6 BDB books ago. Her stories are heavy on the romance and graphic sex, but more than that, each book builds on a huge war that gets more and more involved with each installment. To miss even one book in sequence is to miss A LOT of pieces to the overall puzzle.

And even having gay and lesbian friends, I hadn't really thought about what a M/M relationship in one of my favorite series would mean ... would I love it? Hate it? A few threads on Ward's forums spoke of other readers wondering the same thing. A few suggestions were offered up by long-time readers of M/M ... the most common being the Special Forces serial by Marquesate. They did warn about the violent, graphic, and realistic nature of the military so I set those aside for the time being and went in search of something a little less involved, those having been updated regularly over years.

On March 9th I bought *Strongman* by Denise Rossetti ... followed immediately by Claire Thompson's *Polar Reaction*. And then I was off and running, spending over $300 in the first month alone ... $1.49-$4.99 at a time. It was just so easy to click and read that I had no idea how much I spent collectively until I was totaling out my bills at the end of the month. O.o

And I hadn't told anyone what I was reading. Every author was a new author to me, and I had no idea about the difference between gay romances and gay erotica and which authors wrote which sub-genre. And as my luck would have it, just as the "Fuck's" started flying, someone would poke their head in or ask me a question, sometimes standing right behind me before I even knew they were there. Each time was like a jolt to my system, heart racing and my face immediately flushing; I know I looked guilty somehow. And it wasn't so much the gender of the characters but all the graphic sex talk and cursing. I have a Kindle now, but at the time, I read on my computer and the text was huge. What did they see? What did they think? A part of me wondered if they would think I was gay since there were obviously multiple cocks involved in what they had just read over my shoulder.

No one seemed to notice my odd reactions, at least never mentioning them, anyway, and I was free to work out how I felt about what I was reading without having to try to explain it. It became very clear early on that I may have had some preconceived ideas floating around my head that I would have quickly denied had I been asked about them prior to reading stories with gay characters. Not prejudices, exactly ... but certainly naïve, un-enlightened, and possibly offensive ideas because "having a gay friend/relative" can't be anything close to actually being gay. With each new story, I was uncovering subconscious thoughts and reconciling them with a new understanding; actually thinking instead of assuming.

My reactions at being "discovered" had certainly calmed now that I was more comfortable and certain in my beliefs and eventually, I began telling people ... my sister, my aunt, my dad, a few friends. And during the months that followed I read. Some of my favorites are still some of the earliest stories I read. Maybe it's just the memories of discovering the genre, but I still pull up those first reads and smile as I read them for the 20th time.

◆ ◆ ◆

P.L.

You know, it's been so long, that I'm not exactly sure I can pinpoint where I first encountered it. I'm going to say probably Mink's Ronin Cake archive, a Yaoi Ronin Warriors site.

What attracts you and why do you think it does?

I've read quite a lot of hetero romance, which I also enjoy, but there's something that I enjoy about two males being cast in the romantic roles. I don't particularly enjoy gay porn—something about real life just not being as attractive as fictional characters that I can create the images of in my own head, or the ones I draw which of are often pretty enough to be androgynous. It's the fantasy of it.

♦   ♦   ♦

Teresa

I've always been an avid reader but my passion is for ménage stories. While I enjoyed them, they were all the typical m/f/m with no touching between the guys or accidental touches that were glossed over. I'd never thought anything about this or questioned it until I read *Passionate Realities* by Nicole Austin. This one started out normal but there was one difference because Cass encouraged the guys to be open to more than just her in their relationship. I really loved that in the f/m/m scene, she not only encouraged them but also made sure they both knew she loved them for expressing their love towards each other physically.

The light bulb went off and I realized that this was what I was missing. I want books that showed all parties touching and loving each other, not one getting the attention of two all the time. I wanted to read about guys touching each other, without weirdness or awkwardness, as well as the girl so I went off searching. I found another book with a gay couple who bring a girl into their relationship. Now this was my first book with an established gay couple, even if they wanted their third to be female, and I really enjoyed reading about them and realized I could probably find more stories with just guys so I went looking.

♦   ♦   ♦

Helen

I first discovered gay male romance by accident. I had been after a specific Ellora's Cave book for quite a while and back then my only option to buy the book was on eBay but I never won the auctions. Then I discovered eBooks and decided to check the Ellora's Cave website to see if the book I wanted was available as an eBook. When the website came up on my screen it had that week's new releases on the front page. I skimmed through them and one of the books caught my eye and sounded intriguing so I clicked on it to read the full blurb. The book was *Open to*

Possibilities by Carol Lynne.

My first reaction was – Wow I didn't know stories about gay men even existed; do I really want to read them? I did ponder this question for quite a while, maybe a day or two. The thing that got me to press that buy button for my first gay romance was the story, not the orientation of the characters involved. I really liked the sound of that story and wanted to read it. The cover was pretty hot too, I'm sure that influenced my decision in some not so small way. I figured that for the small cost of an eBook as opposed to buying a print book like I was used to doing would be a good way to read the book and if I didn't like it then it would only be a couple of bucks wasted. I read the book and loved it, much to my surprise because I thought it might squig me out. I loved it so much that two days later I bought the first two books in the series and haven't missed one of Carol's books since then. After that I went hunting for more.

◆　◆　◆

Elisa

I think I have to split this question in Gay Romance and Gay Fiction. I have always had an interest in Gay Fiction from the moment I discovered *Maurice* by E.M. Forster. At first it was an interest more focused on Gay Movies, I still remember when I first saw *The Boys in the Band, Torch Song Trilogy, Philadelphia,* and the more recent movies, *Trick* and *Jeffrey* (btw these two are my favorites since they are romance with a happily ever after or an happily for now). Among those movies there was *Maurice* directed by James Ivory, and since I was also an eager reader, and the English masters were among my favorites, of course I wanted to read the novel by Forster. This novel was translated into Italian, but not so many other novels with a gay theme were available, so I remember I bought the novella by Annie Proulx (years before it was adapted for the screen), but after that I didn't find any other book. I continued to go and see all the movies I could find, but on the literary field it would be years before I read another novel.

Romance was my other love, I have always read a lot of

romances, but only few of the very good romances were translated into Italian, and so I joined an Italian Yahoo group devoted to romance and to the promotion of authors who were not available into Italian translation. Another woman in the group proposed *Crossing the Lines* by Stephanie Vaughn but the reaction she received was quite disconcerting, she was really treated like she was a pervert, especially since the book was an erotic romance, and other women didn't understand why they had to read about men having sex. My reaction was instead of curiosity, first since I didn't know such romances were available, and second since this side of the gay life didn't scare me, actually what I always really enjoyed were the gay love stories, both in novels and movies, and sex is part of love. I read that novel and I loved it so much I bought all the M/M romances by the same publisher, and then by other publishers with the same authors, and then by other publishers, and then... it was an addiction.

Often I go back and think why I became addicted, what it was that is pushing me to always read more and more. If not for the fact that my first love for gay movies and novels goes back to when I was a teenager, I would have said it was due to one of my "failed" love stories: I fell in love with a gay man, but instead of reacting like it was a betrayal (he didn't tell me until I didn't sum it up by myself), I have always wished him to be happy, and so maybe I'm searching his happily ever after in these stories. But as I said, this man came later in my life, when I was in my twenties, but Maurice and Annie Proulx were years before that.

A second theory was the "Laura Kinsale" theorem: Laura Kinsale wrote in an essay on romance (Dangerous Men and Adventurous Women) that the female reader identifies herself in the hero and not in the heroine, and that is the reason why the hero is so strong in the romance novel in comparison to the heroine. If I adapt this concept to the M/M romance, there is no problem of identification, the female reader can pick both heroes without having to choose and she is not annoyed by the weak heroine. This could be a good explanation for me, woman in career, not married, without children and with no desire to have them, but that is what I'm now and not what I was in my teen years, or my inner self was already strong in that age to be able to influence my reading choices, or there was something else, that I'm not really able to frame.

◆　◆　◆

Sheri

I discovered Gay Romance at one of our mainstream book club meetings. Friends were whispering about a book that they just finished, and being the curious, nosey person that I am, I asked. I just finished reading Black Dagger Brotherhood by J.R Ward and Anita Blake series by Laurell K Hamilton, and they both had some gay scenes which were exciting so I was game to try something new. At first, I hid it from my husband, not wanting him to misunderstand why I was reading men getting it on with other men. Most love stories are happy, fluffy and sappy, but men with men can be all that with a primal roughness that is very hot and sexy. I guess the first thing that went through my head was "holy cow, you can do that!"

◆　◆　◆

Jen

I read J.R. Ward's Black Dagger Brotherhood series, and was immensely disappointed when Butch and V didn't get together – I felt betrayed and totally let down. I thought she sold out and bowed to societal pressure. Around the same time, I read the storyline about Jules and Robin from Suzanne Brockmann's series of SEAL operatives, and fell in love with them. When I finished the story Suzanne wrote about their wedding, I knew there had to be more along the line of these gay love stories, and found ebooks. I had been thrilled to find the wedding story and the continuation of Jules' and Robin's life, so when I suddenly found all these inexpensive ebooks with great gay romances stories, I went wild. I now have a collection of over 6,000 gay romances … and still growing.

How long have you been reading this genre for now? What do you enjoy so much about this category of romance? What attracts you to it and what makes you want more?

I started reading het romances during college as an escape from real life because I could count on the happily ever afters, but was pretty tired of the same ol' story lines by the time I was in my forties. I've been reading pretty much only gay romance (and some erotica) since 2006 or so. My husband tells me I have no clue about real life any more, but I disagree; I get enough knowledge of the news through the work I do.

Once I found gay romances, suddenly there was a whole world out there that I knew nothing about, and yet I felt so much affinity with the characters. They might have been men, but they still wanted what I wanted as a woman: a permanent, loving, happy, safe, equal relationship with a partner who valued me as much as I valued him. What's so strange about that? I don't think I ever really felt that the man and woman were equal partners in the heterosexual romances. I just realized that while writing this.

I continue to read gay romances for a couple of reasons: 1) because I crave reading them (which probably isn't normal, but oh well, it makes me very happy), and 2) research. At least that's what I tell everyone. Actually, I learned much of what I know about gay sex and life from reading these stories, although since then I definitely have had input from gay friends, once I befriended some. That took a little work.

What will keep me reading gay romance well into the future, and what originally fascinated me, is that there are so many more issues in addition to the usual relationship angst that gay men face—coming out (or not), families, religion, impact of location, societal "norms", types of gay men, sexual practices, occupation, the usual genres of any romance story (e.g., historic, paranormal), etc.—that there is an infinite number of potential story lines. And many, many more emotional points in a story that make them so much more poignant to me.

I inherited the ability to cry at the drop of a hat from my grandmother, and I can rarely read a gay romance without some tears shed. Not that I want to cry, but it's the sentiment and the actual physical reactions I get when I read a well-written story.

My stomach actually curls or something if there's a tender (or really hot) moment when two men finally kiss or make love for the first time, and I never got that reaction when reading het romance. I think it's because of my perception that men are generally less emotional and more stoic than women, at least in my experience, so it makes it that more touching when it's two men finding happiness and joy. I can't get enough of it!

And, well, two men together is just plain sexy to me. I always say one man is hot, two men are WAY hotter. It's not original but it says it all! LOL

◆ ◆ ◆

Ro

Discovered quite by accident while browsing Ellora's Cave publishing, I found Male of the Species by Kate Steele. My first reaction reading the sex scenes was Whoa this is hot! The scenes answered the questions I was too shy to ask out loud. Then I began to see the underlying struggles of the characters, abused and stripped of their dignity all because of their sexuality. It is the same as hating someone who is born black. We cannot choose our genetic makeup, if we could, then I would have longer legs and perky boobs.

You mentioned some scenes answering questions you were too shy to ask. What kind of questions?

I had heard terms like rimming, toss the salad, fudge packer. I was working at a bank, several of my customers were gay, for some reason men felt comfortable talking to me, gay or straight, it didn't seem to matter, maybe because I laughed at their silly jokes. One of my customers owned a gay bar that served food, whenever one of my favorites was on the menu, I would hot foot it over to the bar (my lunch was always free because they like me) anyway, I learned all kinds of words with no meaning to me, since I did not want to appear dumb, I never asked for details. One day a co-worker dared me to go into the back room of the adult book store which was across the street. After work I put on my sunglasses and went in. The store had all kinds of sex books and toys. I was too chicken to actually buy the "dirty" books, so I bought a playgirl magazine instead.

Did you have a natural curiosity to want those questions answered?

Yes, I never thought of a person's sexuality, for me I looked at the personality. If we had things in common, books, music, hobbies, jokes then I considered those people as a friend. It was only when I started working at IRS (1987) that I became aware of the gay vs. straight issues. "Don't Ask Don't tell" really got my attention. You see, our security guards were all former military, most were Marines (talk about eye candy) some days my eyes almost crossed. Of course I made friends with as many as possible, in the interest of safety. (In case of a hostile attack, my strong buff buddies would rescue me first) Back to the stupid law, one of the guards had been a medic discharged from the Marines because he was gay, I was outraged, since when does a bullet stop and ask "are you gay or straight?" What difference does sexuality make when you need medical treatment to save your life.

◆   ◆   ◆

Wave

Wave, you run a website dedicated to gay romance that's gained 3.8 million followers in 3 years. What is it you love about this category of gay romance?

I enjoy reading about gay men in romantic relationships who are relatively equal, so there isn't usually the male/female dynamic of the helpless TSTL (too stupid to live) damsel in distress waiting to be rescued by the swashbuckling hero. Instead, the guys "rescue" themselves as there is no "gurl" in bed with them (hopefully). Sure, no two men are exactly alike, but under most circumstances they are more pragmatic in solving their relationship problems. They do have issues they have to resolve within 200 - 300 pages and many times the grand finale doesn't seem believable, but hey, it's fun watching the protagonists squirm as they try to fix their screw ups.

Other than the characterizations, what attracts me to the genre is how complex some of the plots are. I love adventures where one MC flies off to other cities around the world to solve crimes or alternatively, just spends the weekend with the hot man he met at a club a few nights ago that he can't resist. What could be more romantic than making out on the kitchen counter because you can't make it to the bedroom? How about making love on the beach late at night, on the baseball field when no one's around … sorry, where was I?

What do you think needs to change or improve?

For years other readers and I have been asking for more diverse characters, and M/M authors are starting to deliver, but there's a ways to go. Three years ago there were hardly any physically challenged, ethnic MCs, any protagonist who was older than 35, or an MC whose religion was not of the Christian faith. Kudos to our authors because now we're getting stories that many of us who do not fit the typical profile of a "romance" reader can relate to. However, although I love hot twenty-something heroes as much as the next reader it might be a good idea if a few more heroes looked like the typical guy you would meet on the street, or the guy next door (no, I don't mean the one who had a fight with hygiene and he won, or the guy with the huge belly, as that is so unromantic in a protagonist). 5% more regular everyday guys would be great – I'm not greedy. Remember that an unending diet of the same character type, no matter how much you love them, gets wearing. BTW instead of throwing away those celluloid heroes please send the hot young studs to my address for an evening of "let's play hide the sausage". lol

◆　◆　◆

CHAPTER THREE
ACHIEVING 'MISSION ACCOMPLISHED'

As a gay man writing gay fiction, I don't have to step too far from the tree to collect a few juicy apples. I'm gay, so I live and breathe the thoughts and emotions of my gay characters. I know what goes through a guy's head at the moment of attraction, I know what turns a man on, and I know how often a gay guy thinks about sex (which is pretty much all the time). But how does a straight woman do it?

It's a fact that the majority of authors in the gay male romance category are women, mostly straight. So how do these female writers get into the heads and hearts and raging libidos of their gay male characters? What inspires them? And how does a female cover artist design a cover that will appeal to both gay men and straight women? Without having been through life as a gay man, how do these writers and artists know what it feels like to come out, to be discriminated against, and to find love in places where love can sometimes be hard to find? And without the right anatomical play tools, how do they know what hits the thrill-switch?

◆　◆　◆

Carol

You've written over 125 titles that include romance, erotica, gay and menage. That's a truly impressive number of books! When did you start writing gay erotica and romance? Had you written anything before that? What ignited such a prolific number of works?

I wrote my first ever book in June of 2006. In July I submitted it to Ellora's Cave, not realizing that I was taking a huge risk. I think it boils down to, I had absolutely nothing to lose and everything to gain. In October of that year, on my 41st birthday,

I received an email offering me a contract. That book, *Branded by Gold*, was a M/M/F, something I hadn't run across at the time. The idea of a book with two men who loved each other as well as a woman, stuck in my head one day and wouldn't leave. I searched my limited resources at the time and finally decided to just sit my ass down and write it myself. Six years later, I cringe at the grammar and structure of the book, but I'm still in love with the story.

By the time my first book was released in February of 2007, I'd written and contracted about eight more. Gosh, my life was so very different then. My only moments of happiness came when I was buried deep in a story. It became an addiction, of sorts. Writing made me feel like I wasn't the loser my husband told me I was. It gave me a sense of self that I longed for. Best of all, I got it. Less than a year later, I was out of my marriage and living on my own with my two daughters. As I'm typing this, something occurred to me for the first time. Maybe my writing has begun to slow down because I've finally found my real life to be happier than my pretend life in books. Wow, this is huge, Geoff. You're like some kind of crafty therapist or something.

Haha, thanks but I use way too many acronyms to be that clever! LOL! ROFL! Tell us, as a female writer of gay male romance, how do you get into the heads and hearts (and raging libidos) of your gay characters?

Man or woman, I think we all want to be loved and accepted for who we really are. Haven't you ever fantasized about finding that one person? All I try to do is put characters together who can't find love because others have written them off as having too many issues. We all have them, some people are simply better at hiding them. I get criticized quite a bit for what they call insta-love in my stories, but it doesn't happen by accident. In my opinion, it's easy to fall in love. The hard part comes afterwards, once the people you love begin to lower their walls and expose themselves for who they really are. It's those issues that I want to explore, that's the hardest part of making a relationship work in my opinion. Although my writing style isn't for everyone, I think there are people out there who feel the way I do.

◆ ◆ ◆

Jet

How long have you been reading and writing this genre for?
What's the addiction, why do you love it so much?

I became a published author in 2005. In the Dark Elves
books—my first series—there were no overtly gay relationships
but homosexuality was a natural part of the elves' lives since
there were no natural born females in their race. There's a
male on male blowjob in the first book but that's as far as I
went because I didn't think I really could or should write gay
romance at the time. But then, in the next few months, I read
more books from my publisher Loose Id, many of them m/m
romance or polyamorous romance. And I met—either personally
or online—a lot of women who wrote them and realized that I
actually could do it. Through prompting from the publisher, my
editor and Morgan Hawke—who I still idolize and who helped
me so very much at a crucial time in my writing—I wrote my
first polygamous story Two For One Deal, and my first full m/m
Romance Snagged later that same year. It was a wondrous and
strange new world when I first wrote the scenes between Michael
and Rudy then Seth and Kyle, but after the first shine wore off,
I was reminded what I'd discovered when I was a teen. The
physical aspects of the relationship were different, but the heart
of it wasn't. From then on, it became an addiction and there's
been gay romance in most of my books since.

To be honest, I actually don't think that I enjoy gay romance
more than straight romance. But I've ended up writing more gay
romance because, at the moment, there's more of a story to tell.
There are so many readers who are curious about gay romance
that I've found myself thinking up more stories just to prove
how fun it is.

As a female writer of gay male romance, how do you get
into your characters' heads and hearts?

Same as I do for my female characters. I really don't think
they're that different. The fact that my characters are male or

female is just another aspect of their personality, like if they're athletic or a computer genius. It's another color that shades the fabric of their lives, another thing to take into consideration when I'm trying to figure out their story.

◆   ◆   ◆

Poppy

I want to know how female writers get into the minds of gay men, and how do they make those sex scenes so hot! How do you get the romance right and how do you figure out what the hell turns a gay man on?

I think getting into the head and heart of your characters is one of the biggest challenges writers face. You really have to let yourself go and dive in. As to the raging libido, well, that's a bit more challenging. One of my biggest fears in writing gay romance is that I won't do the sex scenes justice. So I did what any other writer would do: I researched. I know, I know. Shocking, isn't it? But really, I read *The Joy of Gay Sex* and I talked to my gay friends. I have male beta readers, and one of my best friends always does what he calls a "gayality" check for me. One of the funniest experiences for me was when I had one of my gay friends read one of my first sex scenes. Really, it was more of a build-up. No intercourse, but lots of sexual tension. My buddy hands the pages back to me and says "I love you. But you need to stop thinking like a girl." What? A girl! How rude! Oh wait…I am a girl…Hmm. Then he says, "For a gay man, a blow job is like a handshake. Think about that, and try again." So I did. And when he read the next take, he grinned and told me he needed to excuse himself for a bit. Epic win. But seriously, I don't think a writer always has to "write what you know" but you do have to "know what you write". That means taking the time to research, to ask questions, to have someone else take a look at what you're doing and give you a reality check. I'd also like to add that I think this is true for whatever genre you're writing…it's not just gay romance!

What scene is easier to write—a romantic candlelit dinner

*between two men or two men going hell for leather in the bed-
room?*

Is this a trick question? I'm going to say yes. What? Yes is a
perfectly legitimate answer. Sort of. Okay, not really. Here's the
thing, I think what makes a scene hard is when you aren't in the
right mindset of your characters. What's going on at that romantic
dinner? Capturing true intimacy in characters is difficult. It's easy
to just write insert tab A into slot B sex scenes, but if you're
trying for more than that, a real connection between them, that
takes work. Always. Sometimes scenes are really easy for me to
write because I'm in the right headspace. If I'm having a bad day,
chances are one of my characters is too. So, I guess that rambling
answer really means that it depends on the level of intimacy in
the scene. Because sometimes having a meaningful conversation
is a hell of a lot harder to write than sex, no matter the gender.

◆   ◆   ◆

Ally

Tell us how you discovered gay male romance.

I first discovered it when I was searching for straight hobbit
fanfic in the wake of the release of *The Lord of the Rings: The
Fellowship of the Ring.* Do not laugh! You are not superior to me!
Anyway, so, yeah. I was hunting up totally sappy Frodo Finds
Twu Wuv fanfic (because I'm a ROMANTIC goddammit) online
when I ran a across Frodo/Sam slash totally by accident. It was
a real eye-opener. I rejected it at first. I thought, what the hell?
Frodo and Sam? They're Bestest Friends 4 Evah! How dare these
people sully that sacred relationship with dirty buttsecks?

Yeah, that attitude didn't last long. I soon saw the light. I don't
remember the name of the story that turned me, but it involved
a three-way between Sam, Frodo and Rosie Cotton, with a lot of
on-screen sex (and romance) between Sam and Frodo. I know
fanfic has a bad reputation, but this story was actually not bad.
The sex, looking back, was kind of over the top, but the actual
plot was thought-provoking and, yeah, pretty good. It sent me
out looking for more, and set me on the path to eventually write

gay romance. So, shout-out to whoever wrote that fanfic. You are to blame :D

For anyone out there who doesn't know, tell us what fanfic is.

Fanfic = fan fiction. That is, stories by fans, using the existing characters and usually—though not always—the settings and major plot points of the stories on which the fan stories are based. Like any other fiction, most of it is dreck. Some of it is decent. And a small percentage is really, really good. I feel I need to make sure you know that not all fanfic is slash fic (that is, same sex romance/sex fic) and not all of it is at all romantic or sexual. There's a fair amount out there that's just plain old adventure/horror/comedy/whatever. Any kind of fanfic you want, you can find someplace. There's PLENTY of it out there. All you need is Google and a type of story—or, in the case of slashfic, a pairing—in mind. Sadly, I'm not sure what the popular pairings are. I've always been a dork, I've never known what was popular. LOL. But, whatever TV show/movie/book/real-life people you can think of, there's fanfic out there for it.

To be honest, the only fanfic I'm still interested in these days is Harry/Draco. That's right. I read it. DON'T YOU TRY TO TELL ME THEY DON'T BELONG TOGETHER! Jo got the ending wrong!

See, that's funny because apparently there really are Harry/Hermione shippers (that is, those who are, shall we say, keenly interested in the idea of that particular relationship) who really, truly believe that Harry and Hermione should have ended up together and that J.K. Rowling actually got it wrong.

Yeah, you heard me. The world is an endlessly strange and disturbing place.

Anyway, yeah. There's still a crazy amount of fanfic out there, and you know now what part of it I read, even if it's only occasionally nowadays.

How long you've been reading, and writing, gay romance?

I've been reading for about, what, ten years or so? I think

that's right. I've been writing professionally since 2004, when I had my first short story published.

When I started reading gay romance—the non-fanfic sort—I read it because it was new to me, it was different, it was undeniably hot. Just like everything else in life, the newness wore off fast and I continued reading it mostly because I loved the dynamic between two male romantic leads. It's completely different from that between a man and a woman, for all kinds of reasons I won't go into here because I'd be writing a dissertation and no one wants that. Ha.

Relationships between people of all kinds fascinate me and always have. If I'm honest, I think the reason the male/male romantic relationship draws me the way it does, as a reader and a writer, is because I cannot ever be a part of that relationship. As human beings we're always drawn to the unknown and unknowable. I'm not a biological male, I am firmly female in my gender identity, so I can't ever be part of a male/male relationship. Therefore, that relationship is the most interesting thing in the whole world to me. I think it's more complex than that, but honestly? I believe that's the heart of it. Simple human nature!

Also, I've always felt I identified more with the male point of view than the female. I've tried writing female main characters. It doesn't work. They came out either like men or hopeless Mary Sues. I have no idea why, but it does seem to be a fact.

What's the trick to a woman writing great gay romance?

I don't really think of my guys as primarily "gay men". I approach my characters from the standpoint of, who are they as people? Where and how did they grow up? What kinds of people do they hang out with? What music do they like, and why? What makes them sad? Nostalgic? Afraid? What's their happy place? Really, where their sexuality comes into the equation—other than the obvious—is in how they react to the inevitable overt and subtle discrimination out there in the world. And once again, that has to come from who they are as human beings. Some guys let it roll off their backs, even if it irritates them. Others are saddened and disturbed, others angry, still others afraid to let anyone know they're gay. Most guys, I think, have at least some degree of mixed feelings going on. Most of us do when it comes to issues intimately affecting our lives that other people have decided they are going to speak out on when they have no place saying a word.

And pardon me while I get off the soapbox.

In any case, I've always felt that a writer should approach his or her characters as real human beings, rather than one particular intrinsic trait. People are so much more complicated than that.

◆   ◆   ◆

P.L.

As an artist of gay male romance covers, how do you capture the story and its gay characters? Where do you draw your inspiration from?

Most of it comes from my imagination. Google helps with supplying poses or models if I'm having problems picturing something with the artwork. Authors will sometimes supply pictures of how they see their characters, or actors or musicians who've inspired them, and I'll go by that.

◆   ◆   ◆

Norma

What's one of the reasons you wanted to write Gay Romance?

I decided to write a Gay Romance story for my daughter Em who was really sick in hospital. I was told to prepare myself that she might die, and in one of the oncology wards there was this young gay couple. One of the guys had cancer and Em and I decided to write my story Gay Romance so they could have a Happily Ever After.

◆   ◆   ◆

CHAPTER FOUR
INTERNATIONAL AFFAIRS

Culture. For better or worse, it defines us. It can force us to be conservative, encourage us to be independent, put labels on us, make us hide our true desires, or give us the freedom to be exactly who we are.

Family. For better or worse, they define us as well. They can love or reject us, embarrass or enlighten us, support or surprise us. Sometimes we hide things from them, and sometimes they're the only ones who will ever understand us.

In putting this project together, it was important to me to invite women not only with different family backgrounds, but also from different cultures around the world to participate. So let's dig a little deeper and visit the countries, cities, communities, neighborhoods, and family homes of our interviewees, and find out who are the most important people in their lives. (Be sure to wipe your feet on the welcome mat at the door.)

◆ ◆ ◆

Z

Tell us about you and your world, where you live now and where you've been.

I just moved back from a small town of eight million people in China called Suzhou (pronounced Sue-Joe). I am currently living in the South of the United States.

Oh, stop right there please Z. Let's skip straight to Suzhou. What are the attitudes towards homosexuality in mainland China?

In Suzhou, as I have said gay doesn't exist. I was there five and half years and it took five years to find the one and only gay club. The taxi driver wouldn't take me to the address of The

Deep Breath Club. He dropped my very indulgent husband and I off around the block and down the street. After walking for ten minutes, I found an unmarked door with a thick black blanket covering it but throbbing music was slipping out. I took a deep breath and entered Suzhou's gay kingdom.

As you entered on the right there are bathrooms. One to use and the other was to be used with a companion who waited outside the door. Walking down the steps I felt like I was heading into a seventh grade dance, the nervous tension was palatable. All the clichés were represented. The rich older businessmen near the small raised stage, the college boys in back, the regulars sitting next to the bar and the small contingency of lesbians off to one side. We were seated with the outcast zone which was fine with me it was closest to the big screen TV.

As I said pornographic material here is forbidden. You can go on their version of YouTube (YouKu) and see a woman kill a kitten with a high heel but no naked pictures. However, the big screen TV in The Deep Breath Club was playing DVDs that were especially delicious even though there was no actual penetration. It was mostly very muscular Asian men doing exercises and some naughty dancing. The few scenes that included a bed had a feminine cross dresser playing the female role of the reluctant lover.

The atmosphere was smoky and everyone was drinking. One of the fascinating things I have found here in China (and in Asia in general but especially in business) is men drink so they have an excuse to do what they actually want to do. So beer flowed like water. Men ordered four bottles of beer at a time.

What I also noticed was no one stopped and stared at me. My blond hair, blue eyes and white skin (which should be interpreted as pasty) was usually cause for excitement. But in this club we didn't have the foreign drama that we usually encountered, we were simply allowed to be. It was refreshing.

Now even if you have never entered a gay bar you have an impression given by movies or in books. There is an expectation. The stereotypical idea of hot men perfectly dressed to impress, dancing to attract a partner or just hanging out with friends being cool. It is all very chic.

The Deep Breath Club tragically broke all those stereotypes. There was not a fashion plate in the crowd. I was worried the few people that got onto the dance floor would have their 'gay card' revoked for their 'moves' which again reminded me of a seventh grade dance was more like banging into each other as a joke. There were drunken men playing with laser pointers and like twelve- year old boys they were pointing them at other men's pants or in their mouths. There was only one male that one could consider the stereotypic 'twink'. The boy was using his one and only dance move to impress himself in the mirror. It was like watching a bird looking at the beautiful bird that lives in the mirror.

But what struck me after five years of living without anything gay in my world here were men being who they were. They may have been forced into marriage and made to keep their closet door shut tight but here for a little while they could be themselves and as the club's name suggests they could take a deep breath. It reminded me how very grateful I am to be an American.

◆   ◆   ◆

Dolorianne

Tell us about you and your world, Dolorianne. Tell us about where you live, your family, your upbringing, and who you are today.

I live on the east coast of Florida. I think most people would call Florida a conservative place to live but I just don't see it that way. The state has a lot of laws and regulations that place limitations on gay relationships, but very few of the people I actually know have any issues with gay men and women. I see gay people around town and I never see them singled out in a negative way, nor do they look uncomfortable or afraid about being in public. I know there may be areas that are more narrow-minded but so far, so good.

I have a roommate and a neighbor who also read M/M. They are part of the original book club I am part of. I was living with my Aunt, Uncle, and older sister when I first started reading M/M so they all know; it doesn't seem to faze them at all. We've had so many discussions about the books themselves, as well as about the real gay people and issues those books represent.

One of the most memorable discussions involved my older sister, my younger sister, and my Dad. My younger sister, who was 12 at the time, mentioned not liking a show because it had "bad people" on it. The way she said it, kind of slow and quiet like she wasn't sure how we would react, made me ask her what she meant by "bad people." I was wondering how bad they could be since the show airs on a kids network. When she said "gay people" in the same tone as before, I was floored. I think my Dad was just as speechless because he had that look on his face that most dads get when they have so much to say but don't know where to start and the pressure was about to blow his teeth out.

I asked her why she thought gay people were bad and she admitted that a very important member of our extended family had told her that. This person had been babysitting her over the summer breaks since my Mother died a few years before, and had many opportunities to reinforce this thought process. My sister told us of several instances where inappropriate comments were either made in a family environment, within her hearing or said directly to her. And not just about homosexuality, but differences in skin, religion, and politics, too. By now my Dad's face was red and we wondered if his head might actually pop off.

After reassuring her that Dad's reaction wasn't because he was mad at her, we all had an age appropriate discussion about what being gay did/didn't mean and about the people already in her life that she hadn't known were gay. And because my Dad's main hobby is politics, our discussion veered into human rights and laws and regulations throughout the country. I noticed we had lost my younger sister a bit during that part since politics sound a lot like Charlie Brown's teachers' "wanh, wanh, wanh" to most 12 year olds, but she was apparently still listening.

Then my Dad said something that hijacked the conversation again. He asked if we thought that politicians were using gay rights as a "smoke and mirrors" tactic to skirt around the important topics of health care and the economy. Flummoxed again, I asked him to clarify what he meant. He then asked if we agreed that there were a lot more pressing things for the politicians to be concerned with than gay rights since gay people represented such a small percentage of the American population, and that once some of the larger issues were addressed then politicians could take up smaller causes. Knowing he didn't mean as it no doubt sounded, my response was just a definitive "no" instead of the "NOOOOO" I wanted to scream. My older sister and I had already had several conversations about this in the past and she was right there with me by offering up story after story about bullying, suicides, unfair and inhumane treatment in all things legal and medical, people who were miserable and hiding who they were because of society's insecurities. My little sister was horrified when she heard about other kids her age and my Dad was appalled as we showed him website after website with cases of the same separate-but-equal treatment that he vehemently disagreed with from the civil rights movement of the 50s and 60s. He discovered the difference between a civil union/partnership and a marriage, read the fine print of DOMA and DADT, and heard from kids raised by same-sex parents. He no longer thinks of gay rights as such a little issue anymore.

And I had not talked to my little sister about gay rights prior to that because I was blind to the fact that she was getting older and I just figured she was too young to understand. The sexual volume of the books I was reading wasn't age appropriate so it never crossed my mind to talk to her about them, either. All that changed after that full day, family fun-fest. By not bringing it up, and by keeping my printed copies with two men embracing on the covers tucked out of her sight, I was applying a stigma without realizing it. I learned that the more the younger kids see healthy, age appropriate affection between adults regardless of gender, the better. Hopefully it means they will never even think to question "normal." And while I skip over the sex scenes, I talk to her about the books and movies with gay themes. She's 15 now and even comes to our M/M book club meetings sometimes.

◆   ◆   ◆

Anne

Anne, you're from England. I can almost hear the accent in your answers! Tell us about the world of Anne Brooke.

I live in a little village in Surrey in the UK, half way between London and the south coast. We moved here in September and I'm loving it, especially as it's the first time my husband and I have had a house (rather than a flat/apartment) and a garden. It's a whole new experience of home-owning. We've been married for eighteen years and have no children by choice, as neither of us particularly like them and would rather focus our energies in other directions.

I work three days a week as a PA in the student support services at our local University—it's a job I very much enjoy as absolutely no two days are the same, and my boss is great to work for and with. For the remaining days in the week, I'm a writer, producing a wide variety of stories, including gay erotic, literary, fantasy, biblical, romantic comedy and thrillers, etc. I also write poetry. I find I need the balance between office life and writing as I couldn't do either job full-time—it would probably drive me mad.

For leisure time, I play very bad golf very enthusiastically, and love theatre-going, opera and of course reading anything and everything I can get my hands on, except I'm not a huge fan of horror. It's way too scary…

◆   ◆   ◆

Veritarabbit

Veritarabbit, my Hong Kong friend. Please tell the world about your world.

I live in Hong Kong, but originally from Seoul, Korea. Korea is a fairly Confucius society, but I was mainly educated in Hong

Kong when I was young. So I wouldn't describe myself as a typical Korean woman. The culture in Asian countries are all based on Chinese culture. Especially Korea and Japan. Korea (I mean South Korea) in modern time is a very much confused society. I think it is still. Tradition is still strongly enforced in a way. Although it is a modern society now, there are still a lot of remnants of the Confucius philosophy.

One good example recently…there was an old man (70's) who scolded a young woman in hot pants in subway, saying she deserves to be gang-raped. Can you believe it? And this woman, she videotaped the whole thing on her mobile and sent it out on website…

I think it is on the edge of tradition and progression… and usually old people get stuck with no way out… but they tend to be really old-fashioned to the point of obnoxiousness…

Hong Kong is a very cosmopolitan city. It is under Chinese government but has a completely different governing body, and from the 100 years of British ruling, Hong Kong was able to develop a very unique cultural atmosphere. The cliché of West meets East does apply here. And the general attitude is of a carefree one, sometimes borderline indifference. Haha. So that's why there are so many inter-racial marriage couples who feel comfortable living in Hong Kong. You might say HK people are very jaded. Nothing really does surprise them. As long as you mind your business, and not harm anyone physically, you are left alone, mostly…

My background is graphic designs and I am working as an art administrator/curator at the moment, so I am sure I could be the mean median of anything. The field I am in is usually where there are many gay men and women, and these are the areas where they excel, i.e., design, art, film, fashion. So I have not actually seen anyone gay get any kind of discrimination. But I am sure there is still a lot of prejudice and injustice, especially the macho sectors, like police and etc. I heard once that a police man who had sex transfer operation had to quit his job, because of the shower room problem.

I have a daughter who doesn't even blink her eyes when she sees two men dancing. I am a fairly open-minded person, and I hope she also sees that there are many different things and people in the world.

◆   ◆   ◆

Jen

You're married, mom to a beautiful daughter, and one of my favorite crusaders! Jen, tell us more about yourself.

Yes, I'm married with a husband and daughter. I'm middle-aged (i.e., over fifty) but had my daughter in my late thirties so she's in college, not married with kids. We live in northern Massachusetts, and have lived in this town for thirteen years. My husband is a computer programmer, and we've been married for 33 years.

In my professional life, I've got almost thirty years under my belt doing market research, competitive intelligence and analysis in the technology market. Most of my time was spent as a marketing strategy consultant of one kind or another. Much of that involves hunting around the internet, putting together pieces of a puzzle, and then telling the client what it means for them, with a lot of writing. I enjoy it, obviously. I have a long commute to and from work (anywhere from forty minutes to two hours, depending on traffic and weather), so I listen to my romances on my Kindle 3, and they keep me sane.

Since Massachusetts was the first state to pass gay marriage, I'd say that it is pretty liberal. But I'm on the board of directors for Greater Boston PFLAG (Parents, Families and Friends of Lesbians and Gays) and have learned that MA still has some of the same problems as other states. I'm proud to say that MA just passed a transgender bill of rights, but like the anti-bullying law they're working on now, there is still a ways to go.

I've done a lot of volunteer work around marriage equality, and became close friends with a gay couple up in Maine when I worked with them on the No on One campaign. They were the first gay men I knew personally, and I've learned a lot from them, as well as other friends I've made since then. All right, I admit it; I'm a faghag of the highest order. And love it!

When I was trying to meet some gay men, I asked A.J. Llewellyn where a good place for a middle-aged woman could go and not be obnoxiously out of place. He suggested PFLAG, so I looked into it and liked its goals and activities (and my daughter told me that they had come to her school). The leader of the local chapter was gracious if not confused when I asked to attend a meeting, since I was not gay nor did I have an LGBT child. I ended up on the board of Greater Boston PFLAG a year later (doing the newsletter, of course) and just signed up for another go-round. And A.J. was right; it was a great place to meet all types of people, and I've become part of a close-knit group of friends who like to get out and do things together.

So these are the most important people in my life: my family and my friends.

♦   ♦   ♦

Petchie

Petchie tell us about your life, your home, you neighbor-hood. What are the attitudes toward homosexuality where you live in Northern Ireland?

My world is pretty boring lol! I am married with two children and I live in Northern Ireland. I am a stay at home mammy, I have two kids 10 and 11. They are both at school most of the day so I have a lot of time to myself, obviously I read a lot lol!

My husband tells me I am really socially unaware! And he is right I kind of live in my own wee world. I can tell you that my friends are all like-minded and our attitudes to gay people are similar. I can only comment on the attitudes of those I know and the places that I go. In my town there is only one actual gay bar but a few other places have gay nights and there are a very few places that would be openly hostile to gay people. The street that I live on has a really good acceptance of gay people mainly because we have two gay young people that live on the street, one male, one female. It's a pretty common occurrence to see either kid to be walking home from school with their boyfriend/girlfriend hand in hand. Also the local girls' secondary school has a very outspoken GLBT programme as they have a number of homosexual pupils. But then in other places here there have been attacks on houses of gay people so I suppose it's still an uphill battle at times!

◆   ◆   ◆

Ro

Ro, I always describe you as a tell-it-like-it-is kinda gal. So tell it to us like it is in your world.

I live in Kansas City on the Missouri side; Kansas City is split between Missouri and Kansas. We are label as Midwest USA but the general social attitude is southern. Lots of churches are open for business especially southern Baptist, preaching hellfire and damnation. The state of Kansas is more anti-gay than Missouri. In my neighborhood we are more concerned about the drug related murders. I grew up in an era when the term "sissy" meant coward. Words like gay or homosexual were not used. My grandpa would say "that boy got a little sugar in his tank" but not in anger, so I was not taught to hate. In my immediate family the attitude has always been "it is what it is". My grandma was a part-time hairdresser, some of her customers were drag queens. A distant cousin was a rent boy after his mother kicked him out. One night "June bug" (nickname) dressed in drag got robbed and shot, customer claimed he did not know it was a man, yeah right! Anyway my grandparents said he could stay with us until he recovered. I have fond memories of June bug who taught me how to strut in high heels and apply makeup. Seeing June bug again years later made me jealous, my 22 inch waist had doubled, my strut is more like a butt collision and earthquake all rolled into one while he was still slim dressed in clothes that were a perfect fit. And a couple of years ago my Mom called me fussing, she said "Sweetie B(she couldn't remember his name) is in the car with his boyfriend who is going down on him (Blow job) in broad daylight, anybody can walk pass and see them, and I don't know why they don't go in the house!" Now to understand Mom's outrage, you must know the source which goes like this, my parents were out in the park after dark, I was just a little baby and asleep when my dad decided to get amorous, in the middle of the action, a cop walks up, gives my dad a ticket for lewd behavior in public. Mom has had a public display phobia ever since. These days I live alone, at my age the only available men are young guys looking for a mama replacement or old guys looking for a live in nurse/housekeeper. I prefer a man who can take care of me in all things. I spend my days reading and writing book reviews. My family and friends are the most important people in my world.

◆　◆　◆

Anke

Anke, tell us a little about your home in Germany.

I grew up in a Hamburg, a large city with the most important harbor in Germany and the people in my hometown were always very liberal and open. Then after marriage my husband and I moved to southern Germany and have been living in a very small village for nearly 22 years. The people here are rather conservative. But overall I can say that Germany is rather liberal with regard to gay rights. There are several German celebrities living openly gay, e.g. the Mayor of Berlin (our capital) and the foreign minister, not to mention actors, singer and so on.

◆　◆　◆

Wave

Wave, tell us about your home city of Toronto. Is it a Gay-Romance-friendly city?

Toronto is also the most gay-friendly city in North America outside of San Francisco. Of course that doesn't mean there isn't prejudice or gay bashing here, but it's a lot less common than in the majority of other cities around the world. Same-sex marriage was legalized in Canada since 2005 but Ontario where I live was the first Province to do so in 2003, way before it was the cool thing to do, which gives you an idea of how progressive we are in some areas. There's a very large gay population in this city and many gay couples and singles have moved here from other countries because of the freedoms they enjoy here.

◆   ◆   ◆

CHAPTER FIVE
CLASSIFIED INFORMATION

"Coming out". We all know what it means. It refers to the old phrase "to come out of the closet" after your bully of a Big Brother shoved you in the closet in the first place, simply because you're 'not the norm'. For some of us it's relatively easy (although why should it be considered so daunting and terrifying in the first place). But for others it's much harder. The thought of losing a loved one because of who you are is not just unthinkable... it's unfair.

So is it the same for straight women to admit they read gay male romance? Is this something they find hard to tell people, simply because it's 'not the norm'? Who knows about their love of gay romance—their parents, their husband, their children? Who have they told, and why? Why *haven't* they told, and why not? And of those who do know, how did they react? Did they blush, did they shrug with indifference, did they want to know more, did they frown with disgust, did they turn their back and walk away?

Were hearts broken, or fears allayed?

◆　◆　◆

Erica

I was very nervous about telling people. It kind of felt like coming out and I feared all sorts of reaction. I knew I wouldn't get shunned or anything, my family's just not like that, but it was the "why's" I was nervous about answering. When people ask, I still can't say "Because I like it", it's always along the lines of "I find it challenging" – which is true, but the main reason I read and write it is because I like it. Here I feel a bit of a hypocrite for writing about men coming out when I'm afraid to do so myself, but at least I get a firsthand glimpse of what it might feel like to hide.

When I told my parents I write gay romances, they both asked (separately) "why did you chose to write about that?" I answered that I liked the conflicts and the subject, and they replied with a shrug and an "okay." That was that and they support me whole heartedly. Mom even wants to read the stories…which freaks me out because, well, she's my mom and I write pretty explicit scenes.

That's not to say that I've been telling everyone about this fixation of mine. My ex-husband always knew and didn't think anything of it. In fact, he was very supportive. A few of my cousins know and their reaction was pretty much the same. Two of the female ones now read gay male romances, and one of the guys requested a copy of my book. I don't know if there are any gays in my family, but if there are I'm hoping they'll feel more accepted if they know I write this and see that people are okay with me writing this.

The reason I told those closest around me was because I was very proud of what I'd written and wanted to tell people. The pride on my parents' faces when I told them I'd gotten a publishing deal was worth it and encouraged me to tell others. I still get that tingly feeling in my gut whenever I'm about to tell someone, though, but I never get the bad reactions I worry about. It feels good once I've told people, though I can't outright talk about my projects with them. I've always been very shy in person and the social phobia doesn't help. But who knows? Perhaps one day I'll be able to tell people proudly without reservations.

However, there are many who still don't know—even people close to me. My grandparents know I've been published, and that it's romance, but not gay male erotic romance. I don't know why I'm nervous about telling them. My grandma's cousin and childhood friend is gay and I don't think she's ever thought of it as anything other than natural. Other relatives also know I write romances, but I'm still not ready to shout out 'gay male erotic romance' very possibly because of the "erotic" bit. I think I'd be able to handle the gay bit with ease, but…

…I choose not to tell the world to protect my sons. I'm

worried that if I tell too many people, the gossip will spread faster than wildfire in my very small town of 3,000 inhabitants. The world's supposed to be more accepting than when I was little, but I'm still afraid my sons will be given a hard time at school if what I read and write becomes general knowledge. If I still lived in the city, this wouldn't be as big of an issue. I know this makes me a new kind of hypocrite, but ultimately I have to do what I think is best for my sons.

◆　◆　◆

Kris

Some friends and my family. If they're close friends they know what I edit and for whom. How did I feel? It was almost like revealing a little secret, a guilty pleasure. For the most part, it wasn't a big deal. My mother is extremely proud of my accomplishments in editing as are some friends. My husband tells me that he's proud of where I am, that I'm continually showing our daughters that you can set a goal and work hard and make it happen.

Every so often I do tell someone else at my day job and I can only imagine that what I feel isn't even half of what someone feels like when they come out of the closet. And most when I do tell them look at me a bit strange and then laugh/giggle.

I am a little "known" around the m/m world these days because I do a lot online for MLR and I do help moderate panels at different conferences (GRL this year will find me in the Q&A sessions with the authors). Now after saying all that, I do edit under a pseudonym. Why? My husband's parents are very rigid and inflexible in some of their beliefs. So they don't know what I edit or read. I just tell them I edit romance.

◆　◆　◆

Sheri

Sheri, who knows about your love of gay male romance or gay male erotica?

My husband and a few close friends from our m/m book club. My lesbian friend from work, Rose, and James, who sends me his gay porn. They pretty much know everything, but my husband doesn't feel too comfortable with it, so I don't bring it up too much. I have never kept anything from my husband and felt a little guilty not telling him.

I was nervous to tell them at first, not too sure how they would react. I didn't want them to pass judgment on me for what I read or write. If I ever finish my gay romance story, I hope that I will have their support, too. My stories are important to me.

Was it a big deal?

It never was with my friends from my book club or my gay friends. At first, the hubby was ok with my reading M/M, not telling me the truth about how he felt. Then after a few months, he told me how uncomfortable he was and, of course, it didn't come out right. We had a very big fight. He refers to them as the other men. He didn't want to hear about it or see cocks ramming other men in the ass and I did.

He does enjoy the fantasy of having a threesome with me sandwiched between him and another man. The man can dirty talk!

Anyway… When I told him, he was surprised, jealous and uncomfortable. I didn't understand at first what the big deal was, but afterward, I understood where he was coming from. I respect his feelings and we worked out a happy medium.

Who haven't you told and why?

Most of my friends from work and my in-laws and relatives would not understand. They are stuffy and holy rollers and I would be cursed to hell.

◆   ◆   ◆

Anne

Anne, who knows that a devout Christian woman like yourself writes gay erotic romance?

Fellow writers and readers of the genre know most about it. My husband does know what I write and is very proud of it, but doesn't know too many details as it's not really his sort of read. I used to play down what I write if anyone asked me so as not to cause difficulties in any conversation. Now I just say the truth—which is that I'm a writer of fiction in many genres and that my most popular genre is gay erotic fiction. A very small step forward in "coming out", I appreciate, but it feels important to me. Most people react by laughing and/or getting embarrassed and their interest in me as a writer usually fades away at that point. I find that hurtful, to be honest, as it makes me feel like less of a writer. Once they know they rarely speak of it again. Or if they do, they focus on my other non-erotic genres and smile dismissively at the erotic one. Again, that's hurtful, but I've learnt to ignore it until the conversation moves on. As you can see, amongst my offline friends I hardly know anyone who reads gay erotic fiction or at least will admit to it. This is why the online community is so hugely important to me—as I don't feel like a second-class citizen or a second (or possibly third-) class writer there.

I don't talk about it to older generation people (though my mother does know what I write, as my husband does, she doesn't know details), as I feel that's unfair and will only embarrass them. Not everything revolves around me and my beliefs and interests, and especially amongst older people I'm careful. I think that's simple courtesy.

◆　◆　◆

Poppy

When I first started reading gay romance, I didn't really tell many people. Not because I was ashamed, but more because I've always tended to read things that are more provocative and, well, I blush a lot when explaining what I read. These days? I just tell them. I've never received a negative reaction other than a raised brow or two. Mostly folks just ask why. I usually just say "why not?" I think the funniest thing for me was telling my father that I'd not only written a gay romance but was going to publish it. I had no idea what his reaction would be. He's pretty much a stereotypical conservative republican, so I half expected a scolding. Nope. I should have known better. Like the rest of my family, he was nothing but proud.

I think a lot of people get the raised eyebrow and "why" response when they tell people. Do you think we're heading toward a day when that won't be the case? Is this genre and its female audience strong enough to tip the scales from raising eyebrows to being considered "perfectly normal"?

I think that's the goal, when the ladies (and men) who pick up romances have to take a look at the cover to see what they're getting because they'll all be mixed up together on the shelf. It's a nice idea! And you know, the women who are already in this audience? We are a force to be reckoned with. I really believe that anything is possible, and I've witnessed firsthand the power of good that the readers and writers of this genre can do when we join forces. I've had this debate in my mind going on whether or not it should be this huge push for change, or a subtle build up. There are pros and cons to both ways. For a lady with as strong opinions as I have, I generally prefer the subtle approach. I don't like to have ideas shoved down my throat, so I try not to do that to others. On the other hand, hells bells, the time has come for change. I hear people yelling "Enough already! Get with the program!" and I want to add my voice. So yeah, I think the female audience is definitely strong enough to tip the scales.

◆   ◆   ◆

CHAPTER SIX
SPREADING THE WORD

So we've met the women who love Gay Romance, but have they ever tried to convince others to join them in their passion for a little man-on-man love? How did they go about trying to convert new readers? And what kind of reaction did they get—curiosity, horror, or delight?

◆　　◆　　◆

Norma

I must admit that I have seriously converted some of my female family members into reading MM as well as friends who had never read anything before they read my stuff. I gave my daughter TD McKinney and Terry Wylis's *Portrait of a Kiss* and got her hooked on this genre.

I just handed my daughter the books and said read this before you complain about how many MM books I buy. Em rolled her eyes at me and said I've read your stuff I've read MM and then I said I want you to read someone else's work – and the rest they say is history. Now she does much of our perusal of books and gives me a list of what to buy.

I think a lot of women would enjoy this genre I mean it is normally two gorgeous men what's not to like. I would say to them don't knock it until you have tried it. And if you need advice on what to start with I would say everything!!!

◆　　◆　　◆

Amy

Would you or have you ever introduced anyone else to this genre?

HAHA absolutely, my roommate brought me over to as we

call it, the dark side :P and after that we're like a 2 man recruiting crew! We now have four others in the group and we are actually our own book club.

How did you do it?

We talked about how much we like it and wanted them to try it.

How did they react?

Well we recruited 2 others, but the truth is we also had others who tried it and didn't like it and didn't continue reading it.

Do you think more straight women would enjoy this genre?

I sure do! What is sexier than 2 gorgeous men rubbing up on each other!

What would you say to anyone out there who might be curious to try this genre?

That I truly love it! That it opened my eyes to the world in ways I can't describe. That just like in the hetero writing world there are bad authors in this genre and there are good ones. Give it a try :P

Without a doubt there is a definite bond amongst the readers of Gay Romance. Why do you think this is?

I think that a common love is the easy answer. The more elaborate answer….. And to draw a relation to something in my real life…

About a year ago my hetero book club got bigger and we ended up not being as close. The correlation I draw is that this is a small intimate community. We all talk on the Yahoo groups and Facebook all the time. We are excited about what we are reading. This creates a bond with people.

Also the Authors are very accessible in this community. How often do you get a chance to talk to more mainstream authors? I know I don't, but I can talk to Ethan Day, Carol Lynne, Geoff Knight, and Damon Suede. It is like meeting our idols and having a relationship with them. This means so much to me personally and I imagine it means a lot to other fans as well. After attending GRL last year, I have become more involved with the community. Regardless of what people say, meeting someone in person and talking to someone everyday on a computer is completely different. Now as I read a book I can say to myself, I totally see that author saying that in real life. I think this is awesome.

◆   ◆   ◆

Jet

I'm very proud to know that I've popped many readers' m/m cherry. Of this I have been told time and again. My Heaven Sent series seems to be a good start for many people because it's light and fun and doesn't take itself too seriously. I have many emails from women confessing that they'd never thought they'd like m/m but took the plunge with my books and haven't looked back. That's an amazing feeling for me.

In person, I haven't had the same experience, but that's mainly because I'm not around all that many people. I've suggested some books to a few friends from college. Some have been receptive but mostly we have different reading tastes to begin with.

◆   ◆   ◆

Helen

The only person I've introduced to this genre is my best friend who is American. I probably wouldn't have even told her that I read this genre if I hadn't decided to go to GRL in New Orleans last year. I knew she'd kill me if I went to America and didn't visit her. I told her what GRL was and gave her three options: I could visit her before GRL or after GRL or she could come to GRL with me. She chose option three and after meeting so many readers and authors that were all so enthusiastic and passionate about the genre she said she wanted to try reading some.

I'm sure many straight women would love the genre if they took a chance and gave one a try.

If someone expressed an interest in trying the genre to me I'd ask which sub-genre they would be interested in and then suggest some authors or titles that might interest them.

◆   ◆   ◆

Teresa

My mom was the first inductee. I gave her my reader one day when we were sitting in ICU with my grandmother. I'd just read Ariel's book *Her Two Dads* and she had finished her book and had nothing else to read with her that day. I gave her my Kindle and while she skimmed over the sex scenes she really enjoyed the book. It was a wonderful story to read under the circumstances. I'd also shared a few funny scenes from different Ethan Day books with her and sometimes I had to remind her to give the kindle back. We did a road trip once and that was when I introduced her to my audio books, kept her busy the whole way home, and she couldn't skip the sex scenes, which she later admitted were good. Now whenever I get new paperbacks I usually end up losing them to her first.

I've got a friend at work who complained one day of having nothing to read. She had asked earlier about the book I was reading so I pulled up the book and excerpt for her to read. We got to talking about how I got started reading gay romance and how many authors I now read. Since she doesn't have an e-reader I asked if she wanted to read one of my paperbacks and when she said yes I brought her my two Dracul's Revenge series books. The next day we talked a bit and she mentioned that she was really enjoying the book but had been surprised by the detailed sex scene, not bothered by it but just didn't think they'd go into such details. She was also fascinated by the authors being women and writing about gay men. We talked a bit and once you got down to it they are no different from other erotic books on the market, just that it's a same sex couple.

◆   ◆   ◆

Tracy

One of the nicest experiences that I had was sharing gay

romance with my friend who didn't know they existed. He knew of the erotica, the porn and the serious novels, but none of the fun, HEA romance. When I told him, he was kind of skeptical, but I loaded up my old nook with a bunch of my favourites and he was thrilled. The best present I ever got was him talking to me about the stories I gave him and how much he loved them.

I've introduced a few people to the genre, all of them gay men (which is kind of funny). I gave a friend the paperback books from GRL to read on his commute, another that told me that he felt like there was nothing he could relate to, and this genre gave him a voice, and another who tried and was not a huge fan of the romance, but liked the more erotica-type books.

I think a lot of people would enjoy the genre if they gave it a chance. There are good writers and bad, good stories and bad, just like any genre. M/M, M/F, F/F and every mix in between, if you like romance, hot sex, good stories and happily ever after's, then why not try them with two men? If you're curious, you've already opened your mind to the possibilities, so find a good book, maybe a romantic comedy, and dive on in.

◆　◆　◆

Ally

Oh man. Well I definitely introduced my daughter to gay romance. I don't know if she actually reads it much—she's the sort of girl who decided to read Les Miserables for FUN—but she's very invested in the whole Kurt/Blaine relationship on Glee. LOL.

Every time I go to a conference (and I'm including Fanaticon, the local comics/gaming/general nerdery con I attended twice in Asheville) I've talked to plenty of strangers about gay romance. Among those who weren't already salivating fans, some people knew it existed but hadn't tried it and others didn't even know there was such a thing. I have no idea how many of those potential new readers went home after that and read their first gay romance, but I like to think I talked at least a few of them into it.

I have to say that I'm not aggressive. I don't try to push my reading preferences on anyone. Meaning, I don't go around approaching people I don't know and saying, "Hey, do you read gay romance? WHY NOT, YOU TOTALLY SHOULD!!!" I talk to people, and when the "what do you write?" question inevitably comes up, I tell the truth. Most people are intrigued, even if they don't really want to read it. Those who are seriously uncomfortable will find an excuse to leave pretty fast. If I'm signing books, people who are uncomfortable with gay romance will look away as they pass me. Gotta admit, I love trying to catch those readers' eyes, smiling and waving at them in an attempt to make them acknowledge me. Is that bad?

◆   ◆   ◆

Kris

It's a little different for me in that it's almost a split personality thing sometimes. I've been able to attend multiple conferences as the executive editor and I've talked to a lot of people about the genre. It's a built-in introduction to the genre when I introduce myself. It's hard to not know what I'm talking about when as I introduce myself and after my name the first thing I say is "I'm the Executive Editor for ManLoveRomance Press."

In 'real life' (when not talking to someone 'wearing my editing hat') I've talked with some about the genre but don't think that any have started reading it.

Why do you think so many straight women enjoy the category of romance?

They love men – I think they appreciate all aspects of men and to see them in a different light is engaging.

I talk to a lot of people about the genre. Those that might be curious (if I'm talking to them at a conference) I normally applaud them for being open minded and, most times, will give them my card and tell them if they go to the website and pick out a book (after looking at the catalog) and email me, I'll send them the book to try. I've given out hundreds of business cards and I've only had two take me up on my offer (so far). For those curious about the genre that I'm not talking to face-to-face, I'd say give it a shot. What do you have to lose?

◆　◆　◆

Erica

Yes, I spoke about my cousins earlier, at least two of them now read gay male romances. One is my best "real life" friend and has been very encouraging about my writing. She'll read anything by me and she really liked the gay male romance stuff. The other surprised me. Not that she should have, because she's very open (in fact, open enough that I told her exactly what it was I wrote). She immediately asked where she could get her hands on my work. I know they've read my work, but I don't know if they've read others'. I do know that they're not people to hesitate to pick up a book "just because it's gay male romance."

I think this is the perfect genre for straight women. It gives them a great insight into men to better understand them, but they'll also be able to see men in a different light. My own appreciation of and outlook on men has changed a lot since I started reading the genre. Besides, what's hotter than not one, but two men in love? I think they'd come flocking if they'd learn that it's not just erotic books without plots, that there's actually an array of genres inside this genre, from sweet handholding to hard core sex and everything in between.

To someone curious about the genre I'd recommend going on Goodreads.com and check out the gay romance books listed there. They can join groups that cater to this genre, or do a search (or look at lists). I'd tell them to read blurbs, check out reviews, and then choose a book that might appeal to them. There's nothing wrong with trying something new, especially since it might open up a whole new world. For someone shy about trying, I'd recommend a tamer read with a good plot but with less explicit scenes. I'm sure such a woman would eventually work herself into the more explicit stuff once she got over her initial reservations.

◆   ◆   ◆

Dawn

Oh Yes. I literally stalk *grins* Andrew Grey and make sure to read, review and recommend everything this man has written. My God, he can write some amazing complex, emotional stories that have me run the gauntlet of emotions. For me that is pure perfection in a book. Well that and the fact he could write the phone book and I would be in heaven. *laughs*

Seriously, yes I do recommend authors in this genre to everyone who asks. I even buy print books and give them away to readers in contests on my monthly GBLT Theme/promo days at the Love Romances Cafe Loop. Plus I plan a summer of giveaways when the M/M Anthology that I am involved in comes out in ebook and print as well.

If women like emotional, rich, character driven stories then yes I think they may like this genre. If curious, I say try it…what do you have to lose?

Reader, author, reviewer… you're extremely dedicated to this category of romance. Tell us about the importance of the online community to Gay Romance, and why is Gay Romance SO reliant on websites and Yahoo groups?

I feel that many people when they hear the word Gay or Manlove stories think it's all about porn, sex. When in all reality yes there is sex but there is also connection between the main characters. Being online, we, as readers, or lovers of M/M stories can show others how wonderful this is, get the word out on our favorite books and maybe get some new readers interested in it. Online community is small in a way but also loud in what they enjoy, who is the "IT" author they want people to check out and more. I know I have raved about many M/M authors or publishers on my blog, Facebook and generally made myself a nuisance in yelling how much I love their books. *grins*

Will there ever come a day when this category of romance expands beyond computers? Will it ever receive a "real world" presence?

I think once the world sees that this isn't all about porn and there is heart in the storyline, then my hope is that it will become mainstream. It is my fervent wish to walk in a bookstore one day and see a section for M/M Romance/Erotic Romance stories. That would be a thrill to me to see.

◆   ◆   ◆

CHAPTER SEVEN
THE ELEMENT OF SURPRISE

As a gay man, the first lesson you learn is the one that prevents so many gay people from being themselves: Not everyone is going to like you for the simple reason that you're gay. Thankfully, the second lesson you learn is that people can surprise you, and often those who you expect to turn their backs are the first to give you a hug. So yes, the third lesson you learn is never judge people, because that's where all the hurt comes from in the first place.

So I wanted to know if my interviewees had been through anything similar. Has something as simple as what these women choose to read or write affected, enriched or tainted their relationships with others in any way? Had people's attitudes to their love of Gay Romance ever surprised them in a particularly positive or negative way?

◆   ◆   ◆

Kimber

Both. People I would have expected to be shocked or to react negatively have often responded in a very positive and supportive way. On the other hand, someone I thought was a dear friend, responded so negatively after reading my first book, that our friendship was forever changed. Her reaction hurt me deeply, not because of her disdain for my work, but because of her total lack of respect for me as a creative person. It was very disappointing and for a long time afterward it made me cautious in telling certain people about my work.

Do you think part of that negative response was in reaction to the category itself? Was your friend judging the subject matter? If so, why do you think this is?

I believe her negative reaction had more to do with the "romance" than the fact that it was two men rather than a man and a woman falling in love. She was disdainful of romance in general rather than gay romance in particular.

What she actually said to me was, "I don't know why you're wasting your talent writing *that* kind of story?" And as much as I tried to change the tone without being confrontational (she is a friend after all), she simply wouldn't let it go.

Do people have a negative opinion of romance in general? If so, do you think this is an unfair wrap? Why do people look down on it?

See my answer above. Romance has long been the maligned step-child of genre fiction, from the writing angle but not from the reading.

◆   ◆   ◆

Petchie

I couldn't say it has had a negative impact but it has definitely made me more understanding of the struggle that the GLBT community goes through. I did have a surprise with a friend of mine, we were chatting and the subject of being gay came up and she had some very negative thoughts and ideas. Of course me being me I couldn't let it lay so I challenged her and while we are still friends now we don't see all that much of each other anymore. I want to say that that made me sad but I am kind of an unforgiving person and it's one thing to have different opinions (I quite enjoy a heated 'discussion') to me but another to be mean and horrible to an entire group of people just because of who they are, so I feel I might have come out better in that situation.

So in terms of the real world (not the online world, but the place where you live), are you the only person you know who reads gay romance? Do you feel isolated and different? Do you think this will change?

Yes I think I am the only person that reads gay romance, or at least nobody tells me about it! Lol I do feel isolated to a certain extent because I don't have any 'real life' friends that I can have a good gossip with about the books and the characters! My real life friends and I do chat about books we have read but it's all mainstream stuff and it's unfortunate because I do love to talk about my gay romances! But no I don't feel different at all, well not in a bad way because being different is a good thing and I enjoy my differences, if people don't like it or me then that's just tough!

How important is the online community for this category of romance and for you as an individual?

I LOVE the online community! They are extremely important to me, when I first started reading gay romance they were a wonderful resource (is that right to call them that?) to have not only did they give me many recommendations of yummie books to read they were very accepting of everybody and they always made me feel welcome even with my weird Priest obsession!!! lol **gasp** **Ponders** Mmmm maybe that just helped!!

As I said before I don't have any 'real life' friends that I can talk to about the MM books I read so having the online community there just to be able to say something like "OMG did you read that scene with Jesse and Evan? It was soooo HOT" is amazing!

◆   ◆   ◆

Z

I lost a long-standing friendship over it which pretty much sucked. What I found very disturbing was how I wasn't aware of her feelings on the subject until she discovered what I wrote. It moved my empathy to experience. It gave me a taste of what it feels like to lose people just for being who I am or what I write. I was upset for weeks (I still am) but at the same time it made me more determined to speak my mind. It made me more determined to make sure people hear my voice shouting equality.

My close female relative was a huge surprise. Her support overwhelms me and makes me happy.

I find it interesting how people react or don't react to the knowledge. Most who aren't looking at me funny start suggesting story lines. Everyone has a sex story they think should be told.

I try to plug my ears... the guys in my head boss me around enough I don't need someone else joining in.

I have a wonderful friend in China, whom had no gaydar when I met him. I happily bestowed this gift to him, which he would use when we were together. He would gesture with his head, "I think they could be in your book." The fact that he could acknowledge that gay men were in China was a positive step in the right direction.

◆   ◆   ◆

Lynn

Some of the people I was reluctant to tell about my love of gay romance, especially some of my clients, have really surprised me. Most people I've talked to are really open and accepting. I thought for sure living where I do, reactions would be negative and close minded, but the opposite was true. I really know who I can tell and who I can't. A couple of the girls I work with think it's weird that I read gay romance, I just tell them they don't know what they're missing and give them a smile!

◆   ◆   ◆

Carol

I have a cousin who stayed with my family almost every weekend while we were growing up. For years we knew he was gay, but he continued to deny his feelings to us and to himself. After I started writing, he finally felt comfortable enough to come out of the closet, first to us then his parents. Unfortunately, they weren't as accepting, but he knew he still had people who loved him for who he was. That's a feeling that means more to me than how many books I write or sell. Knowing what I did prompted him to finally live the life he wanted, but was too afraid to live, is worth every sentence of every story.

◆   ◆   ◆

Elisa

The few people I told mostly surprised me, but as I said there were some bad reactions I didn't expect and who hurt me much. The most positive experience is that I made a lot of friends online, some of them turning into real life friendships, even if they are difficult to maintain since we live in different countries.

But I had a very bad experience; the first group I was in almost forced me to self-delete myself from the group since they didn't want to hear about, or talk about, gay romance. Of course maybe I was a little too much enthusiastic at the time, and I talked a lot about that, but they, on the other hand, were talking about heterosexual romance. In any case in the end I chose to move away and open my blog, and now I have no more contact with them at all.

Your blog has become one of the most important blogs in the world of gay romance. Was this something you set out to achieve? Why do you think it's become so popular?

At the beginning I was a reader, simply a reader. There were few blogs, mostly romance review blogs, who reviewed M/M romances, but not a specific one, and truth be told the reviews on those blogs were mostly the copy and paste of the blurb with a final sentence like "I liked it!", "I loved it!", but why the reviewer liked or loved it was seldom explained. Moreover the books were mixed with thousands and thousands of other genres and it was difficult to pick the stories you liked.

So I started my LJ (Live Journal). I can proudly say I was the first 100% M/M blog out there. I think the boom started around end of 2007 beginning of 2008. Many other blogs opened and closed, but I'm still here. But first of all, why I opened this blog? I'm a maniac ;-)

Now don't get me wrong, I'm not a maniac since I read M/M romances, I'm a maniac since I have an impossible to resist impulse to catalogue everything, to list everything, to check everything. To put in order the chaos that was the M/M world, and being the first in doing so, was a nightmare for everyone and a dream for me. Plus I'm a bookwhore, and I couldn't resist the instinct to buy ALL the books (now I need to resist, since I have a reading list of 2.500 books [yes, it's not a mistake, I have the folder here in my laptop] and I cannot buy all the more or less 200 books coming out every month).

I didn't consciously set out to be THE place to browse for gay romances, but between 2006 and 2009 I probably was, since there were no other specialized place on the net. At the time I had more than 1,500 single hits per day, with I don't know how many visited pages. Today is more like 500 single hits per day, it truly depends on the day and on what is happening around. I'm also Top1000 reviewers on Amazon, and Top Reviewers on LibraryThing and Goodreads. And I have a good following on Facebook and Twitter. So the effect is spread in many venues, it's really difficult to really estimate it with one number.

I'm not an ordinary reviewer, so it's difficult to say why people liked my blog, I think there are different reasons. Old fashioned gay men liked it since it was classy, something I really strive to achieve; I love a good male nude, but I don't like to "flaunt" it, so often it's under a cut. But I did post out of the cut a nude of Roberto Bolle by Bruce Weber, because that was art. Straight women authors liked it since it gave them a resource place, to find out about what was happening in the LGBT world. Young gay men liked it since it was welcoming and not strictly aimed to M/M romance, but more on Gay Romance (that is slightly different).

Classy environment, welcoming feeling, live and let live mood, being the blog and the books on the spotlight, and not me, the reviewer, that I think are the reasons why my blog became so popular, and I received appreciation from many, many mainstream authors and publishers.

Recently you set up your own Awards for this category of romance—the Rainbow Awards. Why did you do this? How big a job is it organizing this?

The only specific award I could find at the time I started my Livejournal was the Lambda Literary Awards, but while it's a fantastic award, it was not really keen on romance. The only available category received so few submission that it was hardly exhaustive or indicative of the best of the year. So I opened the Rainbow Awards; it was supposed to be more devoted on Romance, but as soon as I started it, authors from other genres asked to submit books and it was really mismatching to have romance with general fiction with mystery with sci-fi…and so it became more extensive, more inclusive, the categories multiples, the submissions exploded…Last year I had more than 300 books and 100 judges reading them. Like the Lambda Literary Awards and few other Awards out there, the Rainbow Awards are not a popularity contest, and you can probably see that from the fact the winners are often mostly unknown (to the wider readership) authors, like Kyell Gold and Tamara Allen the first year, Alan Chin the second year and Marten Weber and Fay Jacobs last year. But I was very proud to have also mainstream publishers like Random House, Simon&Schuster and Kensington Books submitting books and gay cult authors like Patricia Nell Warren and Felice Picano. Arriving first when you share a podium with them I think it's a great boost of confidence for newbie authors. And maybe that is the reason why, this year, the Rainbow Awards were acknowledged by a wider audience, arriving to have the list of winners posted on The Advocate.com.

It's a huge task the one I overtook with the Rainbow Awards, and I often think I should share it with some more mainstream organization, but it's not easy to do. Authors and Publishers trust me and I don't want to disappoint them. All the others blogs or organizations I thought about, for a reason or the other were not right, and so year after year I continue alone in the management but with an HUGE help from the jury, more than 150 readers this year.

◆ ◆ ◆

Anne

Anne, tell us the reactions you've had from people to the idea of Gay Romance in general, both good and bad.

I've been surprised at how accepting and indeed complementary the people in both churches I've recently attended have been—that's been very pleasant.

On the other hand, most of my relatives find it very disturbing and my cousin once emailed me to ask me to stop writing in the genre as he felt it was wrong. I'm not close to any of my family (though I do see my mother/stepfather about 3 or 4 times a year) but the email was upsetting. It would be nice, even just once, for someone in the family who isn't my husband or my mother to offer congratulations at the regular success I have as a writer, but I suspect that might be a bridge too wide to cross.

I am also aware that I must never raise the subject of gay men or women to my very lovely golfing friend as she finds homosexuality disturbing, but she's an utterly fantastic friend and, again, is of the older generation so that's okay by me.

Finally, I was upset when a lovely friend of a friend deleted me on Facebook as she didn't want my writing career to get in the way of her evangelical Christian witness. That felt like a real punch to my gut, and still does, as I'm also a Christian (though not evangelical) and have been one for over 25 years now. I'm not even sure Christ actually cares too much about where we put our genitals and why—it's how we treat people and ourselves that count. That said, it's only an isolated incident, and the rest of the Church family, both evangelical or not, have been supportive.

◆　　◆　　◆

Jet

I've really had nothing but positive experiences with people I've met. But, then again, I don't have much patience for the type of people who wouldn't at least be tolerant of others. At conventions and such, I've met some amazing people and come to care for some of the best friends I could ever hope to have. Every author I've met in the genre has been an amazing person and all the readers have been so very sweet and supportive.

◆　　◆　　◆

Dolorianne

As I mentioned, I come from a very large family ... 12 biological and 3 adopted children. In our Brady Bunch of 15,

I am kid 12 even though I am well into my 30's. Everyone in my family are born talkers and you had to keep up or get left behind. More times than not, I got left behind. I think and over-analyze until I drive even myself crazy. Everything I wanted to say was already being said so I was a relative mute for most of my life unless it was something specific that I needed to say or talk about. I became more comfortable observing than participating, hence becoming a photographer.

When I began reading M/M, it was just me, there was no one to talk to about it. Left me a lot of time to think about how I felt about many things. A greater understanding of the gay community, of so many of the real struggles that they go through just by being and I came to realize that a lot of my insecurities were of my own making. I'm not saying that my issues were no longer real or important, but they were things I could do something about. Why was I worrying about what I did or what to say and how it was going to be taken? My family may love me but I am not the center of their universe. They are not holding their breath waiting for me to screw up.

And once I figured all that out, I began to talk more; first about the books and then about everything else. By dragging a few key people into the M/M world, I now have a book club where I get to talk about M/M all the time. I got even more confident after attending GRL in 2011 because there were hundreds of people who I had never met but had this common tie with. I still found myself hugging the outskirts a little, but it was the most comfortable time I had in a room full of strangers in my entire life. I still suck at small talk and chit chat, but I'm getting better.

◆　◆　◆

Poppy

Everyone has surprised me in a good way. I recently had someone tell me that telling folks about reading gay romance must (in some small way) mirror what it's like to come out. I can see that in some ways. I'm really blessed, though. I was brought up to never be ashamed of who I am. I'm a strong woman, with a mind and opinions of my own.

Frankly, I was more nervous to tell my gay friends what I was reading and writing. Part of me feared that there would be some weird emotional reaction. "Oh hey, by the way, I'm a straight woman and I read about the sex lives of gay men. You don't mind, do you?" Would my friends feel like I was fetishizing their love lives? Fortunately, none of my friends have had that reaction. Most of them ask for recommendations or offer to find me adult movies as "inspiration".

I also acknowledge that my experience has been exceptionally positive. I have a girlfriend who, when she told a gay friend about a gay romance she'd read, told her that she was a freak and couldn't have a "real relationship" or sex life of her own and had to borrow the experiences of a gay man because she wasn't fulfilled. It was really horrible for her. I can't imagine what my reaction would have been if that had happened to me.

Do you think that reaction is justified? Do you ever feel like you're cutting someone else's turf?

Justified? No. It's never okay to make someone else feel like crap for their choices. But yes, I've felt like I'm cutting into someone else's turf, especially as a writer in the genre. The first time someone described gay romance to me as "romance for women—by women" I went into a giant case of denial. Sure, the majority of the readers and writers I knew were women, but there were men, too. 'But…but…we're not really writing this for other women are we?? Yes, Poppy. Yes, we are.'

What I had to do for myself was sit back and put my thinky hat on. I'm sure my logic has some flaws, but here's what I determined. In general, the readers of romance are women. In general, the writers of romance are women. Right. Fair assumptions, I think. Then I went back and added the word gay before romance. The assumptions didn't change.

I know that there are gay men who read gay romance. I've met several of them, and know several of the gay men who are authors in the genre. What I've learned from them is that what I write doesn't take away from their success. If someone is looking to read a gay romance written by a gay man, they can find one. Heck, I'll give them recommendations. I have no ill will to anyone who would prefer to read a male author's work. It is what it is. I'd hope that one day they'd open their eyes and realize that the ladies in the genre are very talented as well. It's a bit too close to a misogynistic view for my taste, but I try to let everyone have their opinions…and then I try to change their mind. Hey, at least I'm honest about it.

◆　◆　◆

CHAPTER EIGHT
EXPLORING THE BOUNDARIES

Sex. Love. Dating. Romance. Marriage. Seduction. Spanking. It's time to get a few things straight… in a gay sort of way. Is there a difference between pornography and erotica? Is there a difference between erotica and romance? Where do the boundaries lie and do straight women prefer one or another? What turns straight women on more—muscles grinding against muscles and large fists clenching wet sheets in the throes of passion? Or that first lovers' kiss on a New York pavement crowded with Christmas shoppers as the winter snow falls? And for that matter, what kind of cover do they want to see—sweaty or sweet, risky or romantic, tender or twisted?

Questions, questions, questions! It's time for answers, answers, answers!

◆   ◆   ◆

Wave

Of course there's a difference. Gay male erotica is usually PWP, while gay male romance has a plot, with two (or three) MCs who almost always have a HEA/HFN. While there is sex in gay romances it shouldn't be the focus of the book, but that's just my opinion.

Q. Do you prefer one over the other?

A. Definitely. I prefer gay romances although gay erotica also has its place and time.

◆   ◆   ◆

Jet

I guess it depends on who's doing the labeling. I guess "gay male romance" is when it's more about the relationship than the sex, where "gay male erotica" is pretty much just the sex and not about a relationship. I prefer a mixture of the two, myself. But, then, I prefer a mixture of the two for my straight romances as well. I want the relationship because I like the feelings, but I cannot stand sex behind closed doors. I cannot stand the fade to black. If two characters that I've come to care about are going to do the nasty, I want to see it. If I can't, I'll have problems with the book. Maybe not enough of a problem to make me stop reading, but it will be a problem for me. This has been my opinion since I was a teenager, long before I actually had sex.

Cover. How about a tender kiss and a chiseled torso? Because both are oh, so nice. Oh! How about a tender kiss on a chiseled torso!

Genre. I do love paranormals and pure fantasy. Epic fantasy is my life's love, whether it's romance or not. But I'll read almost any romance genre. What I don't really go for is the heartbreaking angst stories. I know there are plenty of authors and readers out there who live for it and that's great for them, but I can't handle it. When I read a book, I really don't want to be torn apart. I don't write it and I don't often read it. Which is not to say that there's not a certain amount of angst in my books, but I don't think anyone would categorize my stories as "heartrending".

◆　◆　◆

Emily

LOL the amount of sex is the difference! But then again, there is no real difference as they are all love stories in the end. Yeah, I prefer romance to erotica. To be honest I don't go by covers I go by the title and the blurbs. I read anything.

◆　◆　◆

Kris

I've edited and read both gay male romance and gay male erotica. The difference I see is twofold: 1) those slotted as romance have more of a plot to them, there's something in the story more than sex; 2) the sex scenes tend to be more graphic in those slotted as erotica.

Prefer one over the other – depends on my current mood when I pick up something to read.

I think that the cover should reflect the tone of the book. So if the book is more on the hot and naughty side – go for the nakedness; if the book is more a sweet romance – cover up.

How hot can you write it? It just depends on my mood when I pick something up to read. For editing, I've gone the gamut from sweet to scorching.

Sub-genre that I prefer? When I'm reading – you guessed it, depends on my mood. I've got some stories that I've read hundreds of times and they bounce all over the sub-genres. One sub-genre that I tend to not read much of for pleasure is historical. Now for editing – I've developed a reputation for working with authors that like the rocker boys; I also seem to edit mystery/detectives quite a bit.

◆   ◆   ◆

Dawn

I like both really. Some days I need that spice of pure sex and other days I love the sensuality of two people coming together without raw sexy sex scenes. It all depends on my mood. Some days I want pure lust and passion, other days I want angst, issues and romance. *shrugs* It seems my mood dictates a lot of what I read lately. *laughs*

On a cover…oh man…I want a cover to convey the story… .I mean if it's a hunky swashbuckler pirate then don't put a highlander on the cover for pete's sake. I love silhouettes and pretty much naked covers….I find if it catches my eye then I will look it over, read the blurb and check it out. Hot covers are great and all but overall, give me a cover that reflects the book/ characters.

◆   ◆   ◆

Petchie

I think there is a difference between erotica and romance but I think also the two can overlap. Erotica is more focused on the sexual aspect of relationships and romance is about love and emotion and the development of a relationship. Then you have Erotic Romance and for me this is where the two meet. It's got the romance AND the hot sex but we get to the HEA as well. I think that this is my favourite I enjoy all the romance and the love and emotion but I want some smexin in there too!! lol

The cover is the first thing that draws me to a book so I think it's really important, I think a tender kiss is always nicer even in het romance. I am a sucker for a drawn cover. I LOVE PL Nunn, Paul Richmond and Anne Cain covers.

How hot?? Mmmm I'd say steaming! Lol Now I can't say I am a huge fan of BDSM or D/s but I do like my romance mixed with a healthy dose of hotness!!

Ohh that is a tough one I love a lot of sub-genres! I think GFY(Gay for You) is my favourite. I'm pretty sure the whole notion of it is totally unrealistic but I love the fact that it's about loving the person no matter what gender they are.

◆   ◆   ◆

J. Rose

What's your take on the difference between gay male ro-mance and gay male erotica? Is there a difference?

There is a vital difference between erotica and romance, regardless of the lineup of male and female characters. That's why I've often found it odd, if not downright ridiculous, that many distributors categorize gay romance as "erotica", regardless of the heat level. Just the fact that characters may be of the same sex does not, for me, automatically mean the "Reader Beware" label of erotica should be applied.

"Romance" involves a plot focused on the development of a courtship between characters, with an implied commitment that they will be together after The End. Sex scenes may take place behind closed doors, as in "sweet" romance, or be hot enough to fry a Kindle in "erotic" romance. "Erotica", on the other hand, involves a plot focusing on the character's sexual escapades, which may or may not include any emotional bond with their partner(s). Commitments and romantic love are frequently excluded, and by the end, they are likely still free agents who are off to enjoy other exploits.

Do you prefer one over the other?

I don't necessarily prefer one over the other. What I prefer is a truly good story, and there have been raunchy, irreverent erotica tales that have stood up quite well against much of the romance I've read. When push comes to shove, however, I do have a strong romantic streak and will gravitate to those Happily Ever After tales when left to my own devices.

What's more important on a cover, a tender kiss or a chiseled torso?

I'll admit I do judge books by their cover. I vote in favor of a hot, shirtless bod on covers. A really tender, almost chaste kiss probably won't do it for me. If it reeks of smoky hot passion, on the other hand, now we're talkin'.

How hot can you take it?

How hot can I take it? As hot as an author can dish it out, though I prefer not to read certain fetishes most all publishers reject anyway.

◆　◆　◆

Dolorianne

I think the most popular answer is going to be the extent of on-page sex. For me, there are four levels, regardless of gender or genre/sub-genre.

Erotica – the story revolves around sex, usually to the exclusion of any believable plot, timeline, or romantic feeling. These fantasies are meant to entice and arouse the reader. If 75% or more of the story is sexual in either thought or deed, then I consider it erotica.

Erotic Romance – Still heavily focused on the sexual interaction, but the characters, relationships, and plots are more developed and plausible. There is still an element of fantasy, but it is generally more an exaggeration than an extreme. If 50% - 75% of the story is sexual in either thought or deed, then I consider it an erotic romance.

Romance – relationship/plot driven story with some on-page sexual activity that enhances the bond between the main characters without overshadowing the entire story. Ideally, I would prefer to keep the on-page sexual content under 30%, but it could be as high as 40%-50% if the supporting details are strong.

Literature – plot/character centered, limited sexual content (or fade to black scenarios), usually with social, political, or environmental overtones intended to reach the widest audience.

In terms of what I prefer ... I like a plot or character driven story, regardless of genre. The sex is a bonus, and written well, is appreciated ... but it has to make sense. Too many times, there is a situation where the main couple is running for their lives, but is so overcome with desire that they stop for a blowjob. Or it's two guys whose only connection is that they sat silently next to each other in homeroom during high school, but claim undying love after a chance meeting, even though they haven't seen or spoken to each other in 10 years.

My main concern with all of these labels is believability. Sex doesn't equal romance, for me. And I'm not saying that love at first sight doesn't exist for some couples, because I'm sure it does ... but most often time it is just lust that will hopefully grow into something deeper if given the opportunity. Love is a balance of trust, affection, attraction, comfort, faults, understanding, and shared experiences over time; just saying "I love you" doesn't make me believe it. Neither does adding a wedding ring and/or a kid and calling it a "family." I want to follow along as the story progresses so when the main characters just rush along and jump over important steps in building their relationship foundation then I don't believe it.

I am fine if the two guys hop into bed right away, safe casual sex is healthy and normal and fine. But it isn't love. And the "I love you because you are so beautiful" compliments can be nice, especially since it is the first thing people notice and are attracted to, but that doesn't seem like real love either because green eyes and/or jet black hair is only a selling point if the guy isn't a jerk. And if an author wants the couple to truly fall in love over a 3 day weekend ... then there has to be something more involved, stressful, intense, or dramatic to forge that bond than just a couple rounds of sex.

However, I do enjoy an erotic romance, especially if I know that is what it is before getting into it. If it is marketed as a romance or contemporary and I get surprised then I'm generally not too happy about it and it effects how I feel about the story.

Pure erotica is generally not to my taste because I'm too cynical of a reader.

The sub-genre is a little trickier. I love the friends-to-lovers, rivals, and cops/rescue/cowboy themes regardless of gender. They are even better if there is a paranormal slant, especially shifters. I'm not as keen on M/M vampire stories though. I could name a few that I liked, but I can name even more that I didn't care for. Unless an m/m vampire story is specifically recommended to me, I usually leave the vampire stories for my mainstream reading.

I'm also not a huge fan of heavy sci-fi or fantasy in books, regardless of gender. I can watch it on TV all day long, but the amount of background and world building necessary to satisfy my craving for detail is usually too much for me to keep interested in book form.

And since I am such a cynical reader, I don't do either fluffy or dark well. The fluffy stories just seem too unrealistic ... very few people actually talk and act that way, and if they do then it is with a much sweeter disposition than the one I have or anyone else I've ever met. And the dark stories with rape and extreme violence are not entertainment to me. If an author creates a character who has been raped and/or abused, either on page or as backstory, and show us how he is able to work through it and find love ... I can read that if it is well written and specifically recommended to me. But when the character has been beaten down and crushed the entire story and the author has a quick or convenient hookup as the solution then I feel like the severity of the underlying issue is treated as a joke.

◆   ◆   ◆

Elisa

Really I think you can remove the "gay" from the equation, the difference is between romance and erotica, romance is more about the story, erotica is more about the sex; you can have both of them together, but you can even have a full erotica and that is about sex, and yes, for women is a little like masturbation, only of the mind instead of the body. Truth be told, I will not read an erotica novel if not in the intimacy of my bedroom, and that is saying all. I read erotic romance (that is a little different from a full-fledged erotica) but I prefer romance. I can read a romance without sex and love it, but I don't think I can ready an erotica novel without romance and love it as well.

For everything I said before, of course I prefer a tender kiss, but again it depends on the content the book. If it's an erotic romance, a chiseled torso is the right cover since it's right for the content.

I can read hot, and very hot, but it has to be a good erotica author, not all of them are able to write it.

As I said before, since I like the challenge the heroes are facing in their relationship, I prefer for these challenges to be realistic, so my preferred genre is Contemporary, following Historical. I have some kink for Sci-Fi because I like to see an alternative reality, and how a same-sex couple could interact with a different society, what type of challenges they will have if the discrimination is out of the picture (because I strongly hope that discrimination WILL BE out of the picture in the future).

I have to agree that I think your reviews are excellent. Con-

sidering English is not your first language, you have a real eye for subtext and the layers that some writers use in this genre. Do you think some people steer away from romance (gay or straight) because they think it's all one dimensional and formulaic? And to this point, how far can a romance writer push the formula of romance before a story is no longer considered romance?

In the romance world this was always a matter of discussion. I once read a blog by Elizabeth Lowell, replying to someone accusing romance to be not really "literature", replying that romance was the first type of literature. The first stories ever told were love stories, Eneide, Illiade, Odissea, were all most about love stories; most of the mythological narration were stories of jealousy and love; most of the classics, Tolstoy, Manzoni, Shakespeare, were telling love stories. So why the stigma of "romance" being low-level reading? Since people is scared by their sensibility, admitting you have an heart and that you can feel for a fictional character makes you weak, and weakness is not accepted by society.

Romance can be very complex, Laura Kinsale is not at all a linear romance author, and truth be told that is the reason why she is not so famous, but the Queen of Romance was Kathleen E. Woodiwiss and if you have read all her romances like I did, you know she didn't even write twice the same story, spanning from Middle Ages, to Western Romance, to Regency.

Romance is huge, you can span a lot and still being considered romance; I think the only rule you cannot break is that a Romance has to have an happily ever after; an happily for now is still acceptable, but people will wonder if you are planning a sequel to give your characters a definitive ending sooner or later.

◆ ◆ ◆

Ro

For me the difference is gay romance tends to leave doubt in my mind and is frankly boring. The stories read the same as M/F with a name change, I'm left with a WTF confused impression. Two guys without sex is friendship, regardless of what's in the character's mind, it's the act that makes it M/M. Writing a believable m/m love scene requires more talent in my opinion. Authors with that extra touch of talent is illustrated in their stories. What's on the cover is not a big deal to me, it's the artist's use of color, background and realistic setting that gets my attention. The hotter the better for heat levels, what I look for is a strong plot with engaging characters; I want to visualize all of the action unfolding in front of me even if it's a paranormal story.

Speaking of paranormal stories, is there a particular sub-genre you'll read before any others (for example, are gay men hotter as werewolves... or cowboys... or when they're in uniform?) What is it about some sub-genres that you find sexier than others?

I love animals, they are fun to watch, each one has their own personality, and in fact I like animals better than some people I know. I search for werewolf and cat shifter stories first, I enjoy the detailed sexy animal antics (licking animal tongues, furry bellies rubbing against his lover's skin) works for me. The human/shifter emotions illustrated in a well written shifter m/m works for me.

◆　◆　◆

Jen

Gay Erotica... Gay Romance... Jen, is there a difference in your mind?

Yes, definitely a difference. Erotica is just that – titillating storylines that emphasize sexual pleasure. A "one-handed read." That is one end of the spectrum and the other is gay romance. Romance is about the relationship between the two men, and the sex is there to enhance the story and keep it moving (mostly).

Like the Kinsey scale, there is an untold amount of types along the scale. To me, an author like Sean Michael is romance but high on the erotica side, since his characters jump into bed every other page. That's his style, it works, and I read most of his stories, so I enjoy that sometimes.

The first gay romance ebook I fell in love with was *Caught Running*, by Madeleine Urban and Abigail Roux. To me it's the epitome of a gay romance, learning about the characters first and watching them fall in love. Then there's the sex scene that is romantic and emotional, and you just love both Jake and Brandon and are so happy they've finally found each other. (Of course, I'm still wondering about Troy, and I told Madeleine once that I'm also still waiting for the sequel. She made no promises, unfortunately.)

I definitely prefer romances, can't you tell? And the sex has to be part of the story and not just thrown in there to make it "better." And I can take it as hot as you can write it.

Which is not what I'm saying Sean Michael does, BTW. His characters are hot, horny men and since I read both the Velvet Glove and Jarhead stories, the sex is a major component of the story, almost like another character. You buy his stories, and you know what you're getting. But he can also write emotional characters and has always shown the love between Rig, Rock and Dick, which is why I still read them even though I no longer purchase many BDSM books. Which leads into genres.

My absolute favorite is contemporary, and I love any stories that involve doctors, mysteries (my absolute favorite!), cowboys, cops/PIs, firemen/EMTs, etc. I've been collecting gay mysteries for a long time too.

I also read many of the paranormal stories, wolves probably being my favorite storylines. I've already indicated some of the stories I won't read anymore. And I will stop reading a story if there are a lot of errors or if the storyline isn't going anywhere. It doesn't have to be long to be good! Something needs to always be happening.

To me, it's not the 'kind' of gay man that makes him sexy. It's the man himself and his wants and desires and ability to change his life that makes him sexy. So if he's a werewolf or a doctor or both, I don't care, as long as he's realistic and has a story to tell.

◆　◆　◆

Amy

This is a tough one. I started with Jarheads (a series by Sean Michael), which is pure erotica. One of the things I really believe about true erotica, and in this case, about Jarheads, is that if it is written well you feel the emotion through the sex. I have read erotica that is fluff and erotica that is deep and heart wrenching. Gay male romance is different in that the story and plot are there, there just so happens to be a love story.

Do you prefer one over the other?

No, I don't, but let me follow that with, I primarily read gay male romance because the quality of the work is better. There aren't that many great erotica novels out there.

When it comes to erotica, how high would you want us to turn up the steam?

I can take it as hot as you can give it. The only thing that I find in a lot of gay erotica and romance is, the plot of rape being used excessively with no basis or story behind it. If the rape is an integral part of the story, I am actually ok with that. What I don't like is when it is thrown in a novel as a plot thickener or an afterthought.

◆　◆　◆

CHAPTER NINE
MINORITY TO MAJORITY

Should this book have been titled Why SOME Straight Women Love Gay Romance? Clearly not every straight woman on the planet reads Gay Romance, otherwise this project would be old news. But could a minority ever become a majority? If the women interviewed in this book are so darn passionate about Gay Romance, it begs the question: Why don't MORE straight women read Gay Romance?

◆　◆　◆

Poppy

I think it's a two-fold reason. One, they don't know about it. Two, they don't know it's okay. Sounds strange, right? I think if more straight women knew that a bunch of other straight women are both reading and writing gay romances, they'd realize there wasn't a thing wrong with it and would give them a try as well. Just last night, one of my neighbors stopped by and saw a poster I'd had made of the cover of my first book. She asked what it was, so I told her. She wants to read it. Said she'd never thought about reading a gay romance before. We talked about it a bit, and now she's really excited.

Part of this comes down to the limitations put on the genre. We aren't 'allowed' to have our books on the shelves of the major bookstores, we don't have mass market releases. I kind of chuckled recently when someone said to me that gay romances would never have mass market releases until they had mass market sales. Um…right. Talk about mission impossible. You expect an online only market, with limited promotional opportunity, to have mass market sales. Okay. Sure. We'll get right on that.

As far as I'm concerned, the best thing I can do for the genre is tell people about it. When someone like my neighbor asks me for a book, I'll give her one, then tell her where to go to buy more. Because chances are she'll want to.

◆   ◆   ◆

Petchie

A: It's not helping that it's not in the 'mainstream' of romance, I mean you can't find it too often in your local book store on the same shelf as say J R Ward's Vampire series! For me MM romance was not something I ever even thought about because I never really seen it in the stores while I was book shopping. I think there are a lot of open minded and curious people out there and if they see MM romance alongside the usual het stuff they would be inclined to pick it up. I know that some of my friends would really enjoy it if they gave it a chance.

◆   ◆   ◆

Ro

Because they have been taught homosexuality is a "lifestyle" and the books are porn. People are brainwashed by politicians, religion and family traditions. Most people would rather go with the flow than make waves; especially the woman married to a homophobic husband or has a homophobic family.

Do you think some homophobic husbands might be capable of accepting their wife's love of Gay Romance? Are some men capable of saying, "Honey, I love you so I can respect that you enjoy reading whatever you want to read"?

It depends on the husband's level of intelligence. People "stuck on stupid" reject everything that requires thinking, some men may be intimidated by a wife who reads.

◆   ◆   ◆

Sheri

First, I never heard of this genre before. At 38 I felt I was not sheltered at all. I traveled the world and lived in the most wild cities and still I was clueless this genre existed. I was floored when I read my first gay romance. It didn't matter that it was gay; it was a wonderful story about life, heartbreak, and love. How sometimes life sucks, but like most stories, in the end it all worked out. I like a happy conclusion. I can't imagine that many straight women know about the genre.

Second, it is a very forsaken subject, so to speak. Two men together ... that's a no-no. However, two hot, sexy, sweaty men fighting for domination over the other one, or even a lonely, heartbroken, down-on-his-luck needing love ... oh yeah, men are beautiful and I can appreciate the attraction a gay man feels; it's easy to relate.

◆ ◆ ◆

Elisa

I think they are scared, but this opinion is weighted from the country I'm living in (Italy). Some of them would probably like it, but admit they are reading gay romances is too much. You have to think that in Italy if you admit you are reading romance you are still considered to have an inferior mind, romance equal to repressed/depressed housewives.

It's a bit about the romance, a bit about the sex and a bit about the gay; putting all of them together is really too much for them to overcome, unless they don't have a strong inner self.

◆ ◆ ◆

Helen

It's quite possible that many don't even know the genre exists is one reason. As I mentioned earlier, I came across it quite by accident. Another is that women get teased and ridiculed as it is for reading regular romance novels and told they are reading rubbish. Women who do get ridiculed for reading regular romance would be less likely to try reading gay romance.

You obviously don't think romance is rubbish since you both read and write gay romance? So why does romance have this reputation? Having a son fighting the war in Afghanistan must put a lot of things in perspective.

I've never asked anyone why they think romance novel/ stories are rubbish so I can only guess at their reasons for thinking this. One reason I would guess is that they (the stories) aren't true life stories. I have friends that only read biographies or autobiographies about famous people and their struggles to get where they are. What they don't realise is that even though the romance stories are totally fiction they also show, in gay romance, the struggles of everyday people trying to be accepted by the rest of society.

I think straight men are the main group that rubbish romance stories and they probably do this because they are insecure in their masculinity. They don't want to be seen as anything other than macho men. That's my opinion anyway.

It always amuses me why straight men often act like being gay is catching and that if a man is gay he is automatically going to make a play for them. Straight men don't make a play for every woman they meet, why would a gay man make a play for every man he meets?

Having a son in the war zone in Afghanistan certainly does put things into perspective. Governments and the people should work towards making the world a safe and secure place for all its inhabitants. Every person in the world is an individual and each of us does something that someone else might not like or agree with. Sexuality is something we are born with, it isn't a choice, nobody should be judged by something they had no choice in. The fact that governments and individuals feel they have the right to decide who another person is allowed to love is abhorrent to me especially when there are so many larger issues that actually do affect peace in the world. The rights of gay people should not be an issue at all; it bothers me that my government feels the need to send my son off to "fight" for people's rights in another country while there are citizens in my own country that have less rights than the majority of our citizens. Our sons, husbands, brothers etc are in Afghanistan and the government and senate here are debating if gay people should be allowed to marry. It's ludicrous.

How hot is your taste in books? How important is sex in the stories you like to read and write?

I like the stories I read to have hot sex but it has to work with the plot. One thing though, I don't care how hot the sex is – if it's only being added to spice up the story and doesn't add to the plot it really annoys me. Can a story have too much sex? In my opinion yes it can and once I start reading unnecessary sex scenes I start to tune out and skim over them and consider not reading any more by that author.

◆ ◆ ◆

Ally

I think straight women would enjoy gay romance as much as they enjoy any other romance books. They just have to be open-minded enough to try them in the first place. I would tell people to give gay romance a try, because the only difference between gay romance and straight romance is the sex of the partners. You can still find wonderful characters to love, engaging plots to hold your attention, and an endless variety of happy endings.

Why do you think more straight women DON'T read this genre?

I think if you asked ten different women, you'd get ten different answers.

I'm gonna ask 32 women, so we're about to find out!

LOL! Well, since you're asking me, you get my uneducated psychological musings. Gird your loins...

So here's what I think. Some women don't know there is gay romance. The majority of romance readers—who are still overwhelmingly female—buy their books in stores. Wal-Mart, bookstores, even the grocery store. And while some mainstream bookstores carry a few gay romances, it's usually not many, and too many of them carry none at all. Wal-Mart and grocery stores, well. Yeah. No gay romances there.

Also—and I don't like saying this but it's true—there are women who are uncomfortable with the idea of two men being intimate. I think that for a lot of women (for a lot of people in general, but the question was about straight women), the discomfort is simply because the whole thing is outside their scope of experience. It's the Unknown, therefore they are uncomfortable because they have no idea what to expect. If that woman read a couple of well-written gay romances, or made friends with a gay man, the discomfort would go away because she'd realize that the big, mysterious Gay Men are just people and gay romances are just romances with two men instead of a man and a woman.

It's those who are uncomfortable because they're bigots who are a problem. You can't fix willful hatefulness. Optimistic me hopes that reason is not the biggest one keeping straight women away, though. I really think it's a lot of reason #1 and some of reason #2.

◆ ◆ ◆

Stephani

Steph, we're hearing that more straight women don't read Gay Romance because they don't even know it exists. Why?

While society has made great strides in the LGBTQ movement, there are still many who believe that to be gay is to be sinful and evil. Groups like One Million Moms and Focus on the Family have done so much in the way of hate. As long as they continue to pump out their propaganda, people will believe it. It's a sad, but true fact.

◆ ◆ ◆

Dolorianne

Exposure is the main reason; it isn't widely marketed by publishers. Most people don't know there is a separate genre for gay fiction. They might be intrigued by the gay references in their mainstream media, but it never crosses their mind to go look for anything else.

The second reason is that so many of the readers are reading in secret. I was pretty lucky that I ran across people who were willing to point me in the right direction, but not everyone has that. The genre is still considered taboo and not everyone feels comfortable sharing. There were people at GRL 2011 in New Orleans who had never talked about the M/M books in real life. Some had participated in conversations online, but face-to-face was out of the question.

And the third reason is the actual content. The root of the M/M genre comes from a time when gay authors were writing for a primarily gay, male audience befitting the sexual freedoms and limitations of the day. Those classic stories are not really a draw for the stereotypical female romance reader. As the modern M/M genre has emerged, and become more popular with women, the stories have definitely switched focus, becoming more romantic. That is good and bad. Good because it brings in readership; bad because romantic doesn't always translate well if the story is done badly. Poor editing, weak or over-romanticized plots that sacrifice important story details, and redundancy can be major problems for readers checking out M/M for the first time.

Another part of the content issue is the amount of sex on page. In my opinion, erotica is erotica regardless of gender and there is absolutely nothing wrong with it. The problem is that M/M is too often mislabeled or pigeonholed as erotica. That can be very off-putting for readers wanting more story than sex; they assume it's all just sex so they don't even try the genre, or aren't interested in sorting through the erotica to find the stories with more depth.

❖ ❖ ❖

Erica

Actually, I think there are a lot more straight women reading this genre than we think! I signed up for distance classes in English at the Uni and was in a group with three other girls I'd never met before. Three of the four girls (including me) read "slash" (man-on-man stories). It amazed me, because there really isn't a lot of talk about gay male romances/erotica in Iceland and there are hardly any (if any at all) such books published in Icelandic. Maybe I'll be the one to change that.

As for the rest of the world…I think the reason more straight women don't read this genre is very possibly because they'll think they're abnormal for enjoying it. Icelanders are usually too much shrug-and-whatever to let such things stop them (I'm not the best example of an Icelander, me being so shy).

◆   ◆   ◆

Amy

Preconceived notions, "shame" they don't want to be ridiculed for what they read, I know a lot of women who even hide that they read harlequin let alone gay romance, just not being informed enough. Not knowing it is out there.

Should it be out there? Why isn't it out there?

I definitely think it should be.

The advertising isn't there. Within the community, it is better but even in our genre the majority of the advertising is through people's blogs, review blogs, and Goodreads. Now you know how much I read; I don't do blogs. Everyone has one and it can be very overwhelming. I don't write reviews and I don't like to rely on them when picking the books I read.

Also, the majority of these books are eBook format. You can't walk into a Barnes and Noble or a books-a-million to peruse the shelves and run across one of these novels. You can't look through a used book store or a dollar bin and find a gay romance. This is a huge thing. Until Mainstream publishers and stores acknowledge and help with the advertising and support the community, it will remain obscure.

◆   ◆   ◆

Wave

In addition to raising a glass to our authors I should congratulate the many publishing pioneers such as Torquere,

MLR Press, Amber Allure, Loose Id, Samhain and Lethe Press who were instrumental in getting the genre off the ground and enticing women into the love lives of gay men. They should be commended for the great job they have done in giving us a different perspective of a group of men who have been discriminated against in real life for WAY too long. The newer entrants into the genre, (Dreamspinner Press is one notable example), are carrying on this great tradition. I gotta say I LOVE our indie publishers like Blind Eye Books, JCP Books, and Storm Moon Press whose authors bring a different perspective to their stories and try new ways of sparking our imagination by not always using old tropes. Sometimes we need new and different flavours; not everyone eats vanilla or strawberry ice cream, some like passion fruit. There are many more epublishers that I haven't mentioned but there's only so many words I can take up for my interview before you kick my sorry ass out the door.

I would be remiss if I didn't mention that one of the best things to happen recently to the genre was when Harlequin, (a Toronto based company) and THE most traditional and profitable fiction house in the world, set up a digital imprint, Carina, which releases both same sex and heterosexual erotic romances. By publishing books that advocate alternative lifestyles Harlequin has come a long way in the 100 years or so that it's been in business and this indicates a significant shift in mainstream thinking about gay romances. Now if we can only convince Wal-Mart to sell gay romances sometime in this century or the next …

◆　◆　◆

Kimber

More people than we think probably do read this genre. But like romance in general, gay romance seems to still have a certain guilty pleasure feel that say, mysteries don't have.

By guilty pleasure, do you mean people are indulging in secret, curled up on the sofa with a book and a cup of coffee? Does this genre need to come out of the closet?

I do mean exactly that, witness the growth of the ebook

market. A reader can purchase ebooks in the privacy of his or her living room and have them downloaded directly to the computer with no one the wiser. With the advent of the Ereader they can even read their super-hot stories on the subway without any embarrassment whatsoever.

◆   ◆   ◆

Teresa

I would guess they either think it is something they would not like, are too embarrassed to admit they might like it, or have no idea it is out there to read. For myself I had no idea this genre was available and probably would have taken a longer time to find it if I hadn't read Nicole's book and went looking for similar books. I do know that if I hadn't found it on my own my friends and family wouldn't be reading it with me.

◆   ◆   ◆

J. Rose

More women don't read Gay Romance for the same reason more people don't read about vampires that glitter or female sleuths. There is no one subgenre that appeals to a single gender across the board. Not all women like romance, regardless of who the players are. Some have told me they just can't "get into" a story where there is no heroine—because these women's enjoyment of an erotic tale hinges on putting themselves in the heroine's shoes. And there are plenty of readers who won't purchase ménage stories involving a heroine if the two heroes so much as touch one another. They'd prefer the men to just jointly worship at the temple of her body. There are women who don't choose to read any alternate-lifestyle fiction, be it lesbian, gay, or BDSM. However, that sector of the population seems to be decreasing bit by bit.

◆   ◆   ◆

CHAPTER TEN
TACTICAL MANEUVERS

Men!

Gay or straight, we're simple... yet complicated. We're carefree... and careless. We're easy-going... but stubborn. We're great listeners... when we don't have anything much to say. But... we *are* loving, this is one thing we do have going for us! Well, most of us are, anyway. Sometimes you just need to scratch the surface... or use explosives.

So by reading gay romance, do straight women have a better understanding of men, either gay or straight? Has it changed the way they relate to or perceive the opposite sex? In short, are men any easier to understand by reading stories that delve into the hearts and minds of men in love with each other?

◆ ◆ ◆

Carol

The simple answer would be no. I don't know that I'll ever understand men, but, frankly, I don't understand other women either. I chalk it up to the fact that each person was created to be unique. I never lump people into categories, therefore, each friend or family member is as much a mystery to me as the people I pass on the street. The joy in writing is to explore different personalities and traits of people I've known in my life and mixing them up to create a character that other people will fall in love with.

◆ ◆ ◆

Dolorianne

Definitely. Many of the reasons are already listed within the previous answers, but the overall feeling is that men are just as complex as women are. I find that comforting.

As far as gay men specifically, it is perceived that they don't want/can't be monogamous. I don't know if I truly ever thought that, but I now have a better understanding of why I didn't agree 100% with that statement. Men are stereotypically more open about casual sex than women are. (At least that's how it has been in the past. I would say that as women feel more and more empowered then they could surely rival the sexual desires of men.) In the case of a m/f couple, the man may say yes, but the woman may hesitate. Two men in the same equation and both are thinking of the here and now instead of what happens tomorrow. An instant attraction could lead to more before either one realizes it. But that does not mean that men are brainless twits who can't control themselves. People are attracted to other people all the time, but that doesn't mean that they follow through, gay men included.

Men tend to be more practical while women are more emotional in terms of pairing up. The guy may be thinking they are just having a nice time and the woman has him pressured into an engagement ring. With two men paired up, especially if they are a little commitment shy, then they may be together for years before they realize they are actually in a relationship. Unless they meet a man who captures them right away, then the urgency to "define" their relationship isn't there. They want love and affection and family and to share their life with someone, but are usually not as rushed to start "forever" the way so many women are. And by following that train of thought, men may very well let relationships fall apart prematurely because there were no clear rules which lead to confusion, jealously or indifference. But the only reason it may happen more in gay relationships than in heterosexual ones could be because there are two clueless men involved instead of only one. Pair up a clueless gay man with a "forever-minded" man and I don't see why they wouldn't have the exact same chances of monogamy vs cheating as any straight couple on the planet.

And the last thing about the cheating myth is social and legal opportunities of the past. Same-sex relationships have been highly frowned upon and, in some places, illegal for quite a few centuries. As a result, gay men and women learned to love in secret and to fear discovery. Sex was hurried and probably without a lot of fanfare or romantic expectations. To live together and bring up a family was unheard of. And with each new generation of gay men and women, they've been taught the same thing ... either by older gay men and women or by the prejudices of society. What point is there to being faithful or committed to someone if you weren't going to be allowed to keep them? Better to just stay footloose and fancy free than get your heart broken when your lover gets married off under the guise of propriety. The psychological effects of hiding for so long are not going to go away simply because a guy meets someone who is more open than he is. Some could even go so far as to say that a lot of relationships were tanked before they ever got started. A few states have passed marriage equality, but I'm not sure that the gay community trusts it. Who knows when it could be taken away and that heartbreak may be even worse than all the confusion, fear, and shame they had to battle.

Times are changing so I am very interested to see how long it takes for the myth about gay people remaining faithful goes away as the next few generations of gay men and women are encouraged to love and openly commit to same-sex partners.

◆   ◆   ◆

Helen

On the subject of understanding men, do you see a difference between the male and female authors of Gay Romance?

Who gets into the mind of a gay character most convincingly when it comes to romance: a gay man who may or may not have a romantic bone in his body, or a female writer of romance, who doesn't have a penis but knows how to tell a love story? And perhaps more importantly, does it matter?

Interesting question, I suppose that depends on the author. There has been a lot of interest (to put it mildly) lately on the sex of gay romance writers as it is impossible to tell just by an author's name unless you've come across that author in a chat group and even then no one can be positive except the publishers. Unless I know positively that an author is male I usually assume they are female as the majority of authors in this genre are female. I have no preference as to whether the author I am reading at any given time is male or female so long as they tell a good story I'm happy.

Has reading Gay Romance given you a better understanding of men and how they think and act?

I would have to say no, because mostly it is another woman's interpretation of men which may not be how most men think, feel and act. And to further answer your question, I don't read this genre to find out about how men think and act or to understand them better. I read the genre purely for enjoyment and entertainment.

◆   ◆   ◆

Petchie

Petchie, has reading Gay Romance given you a better understanding of men and how they think and act?

I'm not sure it's helped me have a better understanding of men, I have lived with my husband for the last 10 years and I'm still not sure I can say I totally understand men! (I bet they say the same about us). I do think that it's made me more aware of how men act and my perceptions of them. Sometimes we(women) can forget that men capable of the same kinds of emotion as us, society has all these stereotypes that men are suppose to live up to like, men have to be strong and can't cry or men shouldn't stay at home and be a home maker and look after the children. Being a woman you can be anything you want but if a man wants to stay at home and look after his own children some people look at him like he is less than a man or something! Reading this genre has given me a little insight to how difficult it can be for some men to have to stand up to family, friends and the general public and say 'wait, I don't want to be put in that box'.

◆   ◆   ◆

Elisa

Maybe. I have now a lot of gay friends, and knowing them, more than reading about them, I maybe understand better their world and their challenges. The other day, at the Rainbow Book Fair in NYC, a publisher who usually sends me books to review told me I sometime understand his authors better than gay male reviewers. If I have to find a reason, maybe it's since I'm not so much involved in the story and so I have a critical and analytical eye?

◆　◆　◆

Anke

Puh – when do we really understand the menfolk. No, seriously: I think the only thing that changed was the realization that – although the books are romance and not real life – gay men, aside from everyday life like all of us, have to deal with problems that straight people aren't even aware of.

To be honest, I don't think that it has changed my view of the men in general, but of gay men.

◆　◆　◆

Poppy

I wouldn't call it a better understanding necessarily. I don't think we can expect romances in general to be realistic representations of life. They're meant to be fantasies, and as such, they aren't going to capture reality perfectly, if at all. I know traditional romances don't, so I don't think gay romances would either.

However, I do think that it's opened my mind more to the importance of gay rights. For example, before I became involved in the genre, the issue of marriage equality was never at the forefront of my mind. Now? I want to do anything and everything I can to help my friends have the equality they deserve. Through the friendships I've formed in this genre, and the information on issues like bullying that I've been more exposed to as a result, I realize how important it is to add my voice to the cause. Before, I'd have quietly supported. Now, I'm happy to be loud and proud. Reading gay romance helped put me on that path.

◆   ◆   ◆

Ro

Ro, do you have a better understanding of men—either gay or straight—by reading this genre?

Yes I have a better understanding now. Before reading Gay Romance, I never thought of men showing emotions. I see now it is possible for men to exhibit their true feelings.

Do you see this in the real world, or just in the books you read?

Not very often, but I do see it in real life. One of my male cousins cried when his wife had breast cancer treatments, it was the only time he actually displayed his love for her in front of others.

◆   ◆   ◆

Anne

I don't know if I have a better understanding of men from reading gay books—I think you only gain understanding of people by meeting them in the flesh, as it were. But I do have a greater awareness of how different other people's lives are and how important it is not to assume anything about anyone. I also think now that sexuality and gender is far more fluid than anyone has previously thought it was, and that's absolutely something to be embraced and celebrated.

I also believe it's changed my Christian faith and how I view it. Many years ago, an evangelical Christian friend of mine said to me that she'd come to terms with why homosexuality is not what God wants as only a man and a woman can get married, so that was obviously God's ideal plan and anything else is second-best. At the time, I just accepted it (God forgive me, but I was very young…). Since then my view has become entirely different, but it's because of reading and writing gay fiction and meeting online and occasionally in real life those people similar to me who also read and/or write it, that I've become far more outspoken in crystallising and stating my view.

Meanwhile the opinions of the leadership of my church (the Church of England) about this matter continue to frustrate, anger and grieve me, and I'm also deeply saddened that so many people here do seem to believe that same-sex marriage is wrong and somehow a "lesser" truth. I think they're wrong, and marriage is far too important and precious to leave to the opposite-sex couples. Why the heck should we keep these riches to ourselves for so long and so unjustly? And why should we think it's fine that we offer the "sop" of civil partnership and that therefore should be enough? What nonsense! So I would want to go on record that marriage is for two people, and any other number should have a different name entirely, but the gender of those two people (and gender itself is not cut and dried in any case) is irrelevant. I pray very much that I will see same-sex marriage in all its fullness celebrated in churches and outside them in my lifetime, because God I believe is willing. Bring it on!

◆ ◆ ◆

J. ROSE

I'd love to say I understand men better now, but I don't think it's true. Life does imitate art, but fiction doesn't automatically imitate the real male psyche, especially when so much of it is penned by women writers.

My husband once complained that one of his beefs with erotic romance is that heroes are portrayed implausibly. "Men don't talk/think/act that way," he complained. I argued that romance fiction is entertainment. It is fantasy, no matter how contemporary the setting. Women want to read about what they would love (or love to hate) a man to say or think, not necessarily what they would really do. After all, if people were only interested in the "reality" of sex in entertainment, the porn industry would collapse. Imagine delivery boys who walk away after handing over the pizza, rather than getting yanked into the housewife's living room for a wild round of wham-bam-here's-your-tip. Now, is that what I expect the next time I call Domino's? Hardly. (Though it's damn fun to think about.) So porn doesn't inform my real-life expectations, nor does romance fiction inform my true understanding of men.

Perhaps male authors or gay male authors write gay romance a lot more "like it is", I don't know. But I feel that reading any genre of fiction tells me more about what we wish for rather than what is. Gay romance is no exception.

What's your definition of a real man? Do you expect heroes in a romance story to meet your definition?

A real man is one who exists in flesh and blood outside my rich and varied fantasy life. Ha! My "fantasy" men exist to toy with dream ideals I don't actually expect the real versions to live up to. They are subjected to rigid demands. I absolutely insist romance heroes be gorgeous as hell, endowed where it counts (and I ain't talkin' bank account here), and they must be unpredictable at times. They must have believable flaws and, on occasion, mind you, do something that vexes their love interest. The latter should preferably occur due to a case of mistaken motives, rather than truly diabolical goals.

◆   ◆   ◆

CHAPTER ELEVEN
DO ASK, DO TELL!

If you're this far into the book, then I'm now allowed to use the word *cock*. That's the difference between a textbook and sex book! If I were writing a textbook right now, I would have used the word *penis*. But let's face it, the word *cock* is sexier, a lot more fun, and just feels good in your mouth! It's one of those truly liberating words.

So let's take the 'Do Not Disturb' sign off the door and ask the question that's on every reader's mind right now—has reading or writing gay romance improved your sex life? Do you know any new tricks to turn on your man? And do you ever get asked "Did you learn that from one of your books?"

◆ ◆ ◆

Dawn

Oh yes *grins* let's just say my SO is my guinea pig when it comes to finding a male's sweet spots. LOL

He always asks what I read that got me in that kind of mood. *winks*

◆ ◆ ◆

Z

Reading=Orgasms. There have been studies done that suggest reading romance novels increases the female sex drive as well as increasing the number of orgasms experienced. Some sex therapists encourage females with low sex drives to read romance novels because it stirs the emotions and the imagination. (I have been an avid reader since I was thirteen…)

My writing hasn't improved my sex life but it may have altered it. My husband and I are both Scorpios so we either mate or fight...and neither of us likes to fight. We have always believed in focusing energy, time and effort into that area of our lives. My husband is my best friend and a wonderfully considerate lover so I have been very blessed in this area.

My writing about hot sexy men may have altered my sex life a bit. How could it not? I spend hours a day writing about love and sex. Usually I save writing my hottest sex scenes for times I know I will be able to take maximum advantage of my dirty mind. Who needs Viagra when you have M/M erotica? There are times when I am so exhausted with jetlag sex seems like an impossibility but a five minute gander at the right M/M scenes... I am begging for it like one of my pretties.

Most people have issues. Writing has given me a safe place to work through some of my own demons. I have suffered from severe anxiety and panic attacks for years, while writing about magnificent gay sex hasn't cured me it has given me something else to focus on. When I start heading for Crazy town, I acknowledge it and ask myself about the book I am currently working on. All my angst and energy has some place to go and I get lost in my very own gay playground.

Do you know any new tricks to turn on your man, lol?

Analyzing the descriptive details of any sexual act will make you view it in a different light. To write about it forces you to break the act down in small describable parts. This examination can lead to questioning the nuances. I may have been doing something the same way for years but one of my characters comes along and does it a different way. Seeing that difference unfold might encourage me to explore doing it that way as well.

A close friend of my husband found out what I wrote and he said to my husband, "That's why you are always smiling." And slapped him on the back.

Do you ever get asked if you learned 'that' in one of those books you read ;) ?

When I first started writing in this genre, I may have done something a little different and couldn't help but brag when it was positively received. "That's Darius's move." My husband smiled and let me know later he hoped I continued to write in this genre for a long time.

◆　◆　◆

Sheri

I give great blowjobs; at least that's what he told me.

Oh that's good news for hubby! Has it been this way your entire marriage or have things improved with a little Gay Romance in your life?

After 17 years of marriage, I enjoy it just as much as he does. I love driving my man crazy! I guess for as long as I can remember, my husband has complimented me on how good I was at giving oral sex ...which is nice and quite an ego booster. Nevertheless, it was just a listen-and-learn process; practice makes perfect, right?

Lol…

After finding gay erotica, I have a better understanding of what he may enjoy. Goodness gracious, now I am blushing. I guess I also feel that I enjoy oral sex much more. So, in turn it has improved. It is a major turn on when you can make a man wild with just a touch.

Do you know any new tricks to turn on your man?

Well, yeah, no-dah, I never knew he had a G spot, too! He won't admit it, but the couple of tricks I did pick up from gay romance has him begging for more every time.

Do you ever get asked if you learned 'that' in one of those books you read ;) ?

No, that would ruin it for him, but we both know where I picked it up. ;)

It'll be our little secret then! Just don't let him read this book.

◆　◆　◆

Kris

Believe it or not, this is one of the questions that I'm asked the most right behind "ummm, two men having sex?" Has it changed or improved my sex life? Maybe, maybe not. Kidding aside, I think it's opened my eyes a bit. Tricks? There's this one that I read about that…I have learned things from the books that I've read OUTSIDE of the sex. Most of the authors in the genre take their writing very seriously and do research the backgrounds in their stories. Which completely boggles my husband's mind when I come up with random information on a topic – last random bit thanks to T.A. Chase on bull riding and the bell on the rope (thanks TA).

❖   ❖   ❖

Teresa

Well I can tell you that I have picked up a few ideas that one day I'll have to try out… if I ever get that far into dating again. If everything I've read is true.

❖   ❖   ❖

Jet

I'm blessed to have a very open and understanding lover. He knows and understands my obsession with men—especially pretty younger men, eek!—and he's secure enough to work with that. The lovely man even bought me my first sex toy. We've tried many things just to see. Some we've liked, some we haven't. I do get asked if I've learned any tricks from books. I guess I'd have to say yes LOL

❖   ❖   ❖

Tracy

Absolutely. If I read about something that turns me on and I think: what would that feel like, or how would my partner react if I did THAT, then it tends to become reality, subconsciously or not.

Depending who I'm dating at the time, it may go on a mental shelf or I give it a go, but almost always I'm open about the fact that I've read about it. In most cases, there's a joke about buying a gift card to the publisher of my choice, and I rarely get any complaints about reading in bed!

◆　　◆　　◆

CHAPTER TWELVE
A BRAVE NEW WORLD

We've discussed a lot! While working on this project I laughed a lot, I learned a lot, I cried some and I was truly inspired. So now I want to know if gay romance has inspired others. I want to ask the women of this book, has gay romance changed them as a person in any way?

And just as importantly, do they think that one straight woman reading gay romance can make a difference to views on love, acceptance and equality in this world?

◆　　◆　　◆

Jet

Absolutely. Writing erotic romance has helped me in general because I care less about what other people think of me. That probably comes across bad on first read, but it's not meant to be. When I was younger, I cared so much what others thought that it stifled me and held me back. Now, I'm far less likely to avoid doing something because others might think I'm weird. Now, I know I'm weird and I'm very comfortable with that. It's very freeing.

I don't think there's anyone on the planet who isn't weird in their own way! Being free within yourself, now that's the key! Tell us, do you think one straight woman reading gay male romance can make a difference to gay rights in the world?

Yes! I look at PFLAG moms and cheer my fool head off. I think of women who read my books and have children, knowing that they'll teach their children that being gay is okay, even desirable. The more women there are raising their kids with tolerance and acceptance, the less oppression and fear there is in the world. Because I have to believe, the hate is learned, not inherent. Kids are taught to fear and hate the gay and lesbian community and that is what has to stop.

◆   ◆   ◆

Dawn

Dawn, has Gay Romance changed you as a person in any way?

I am more open, tolerant and feel more empathy for the hardships many GBLT people face each day.

Do you think one straight woman reading Gay Romance can make a difference to gay rights in the world?

Yes because right down to it, they are people like you and me and deserve the right to live their life the way they want, with no input from us on how they should live it. Religion, politics… put it aside because seriously…straight people have been doing a bang up job in creating the mess in their relationships…they don't need to attack another group of people because of it.

◆   ◆   ◆

Ro

The genre has raised my awareness of all the crap the governments as well as the churches are dishing out so they can cover up what they are really doing. I'm always amazed at how many people can't see this. Prime example is the terrorist, holy war my foot! Other countries have adopted the same "target gays" method only with a more civilized technique, bottom line it's all about money and power.

Ro, do you think Gay Romance has the power to change things, no matter how small, in the fight for gay rights?

I think gay romance has already made some impact. However, change will not come until the majority of so called Christians understand their own history by reading for themselves. The Book of Genesis was written by Moses. The Jews condemned homosexuals because they were being ruled by the Romans and Greeks who worshipped several deities. Yet almost every church displays statues of Mary and a larger than life cross and celebrate the same holidays the early Romans did. Our leaders make laws based on hearsay written centuries after creation. It seems money overrules honesty and common sense is lost.

Our Creator loves variety; look at his creations,

Many different species of animals and vegetation.

Heterosexuals, Homosexuals, Hermaphrodites.

No two human beings are exactly alike.

Many people choose to spread hatred and strife.

God's true message is peace, joy and abundance of life.

◆   ◆   ◆

Elisa

Elisa has Gay Romance changed the person you are, or at least were?

I think yes. It gave me confidence in what I'm doing, and it opened a whole world, even if online. Since I still prefer the real life relationships to the online ones, I try to attend as many events as possible, to try to tighten those friendships. I think it helped for sure to let me "come out" from my shell, meaning that I was always a silent reader, and now instead I enjoy to share what I'm reading with other people and to talk about it, something that it was always difficult to do, even when I was reading heterosexual romances.

◆   ◆   ◆

Norma

I think this has made me more tolerant and more pissed off all at the same time. I am more tolerant that yes there are idiots out there and more pissed off because YES there are idiots out there.

I just can't understand why people can't be like me and just go with the flow and let people live and love who they need to. Gay or straight; love is love and who am I to tell someone that they are wrong for choosing who they do. I think the time has come for change and we need to make this better for the future generations to come.

◆   ◆   ◆

Tracy

That's a hard question to answer. I think everything we experience, do, see, read, hear changes us. I can tell you that I love reading this genre and it helps me relax after a stressful day. I love sitting on the train next to the professionals reading the morning paper while I'm reading about two guys falling in love, lol. All joking aside, the absolutely quantifiable change for me was going to GRL. I went not knowing a single person or what to expect. I'm not much of an online person, so I didn't have cyber friends that I knew were going. Deciding to go, and following through, was a big deal for me and I couldn't be happier that I did. I met some amazing people that I now call my friends who share my love of gay romance.

◆   ◆   ◆

Helen

I'm sure it has. While I've never discriminated against gay men and have classed many as friends over the years I had never really thought deeply about what their lives might be like and how they need to fight just to achieve the same rights as everyone else. Since reading this genre my eyes have been opened and I pay more attention to the struggles of gay people. I'm more likely to vote for a politician who stands up for gay rights than one who doesn't. I'll talk out when someone makes derogatory comments, well, I guess I always did that but now I'm a lot more vocal.

◆   ◆   ◆

Teresa

I would say that discovering e-books and this genre have opened my eyes to some things that I wasn't aware of. It has also given me a passion for reading again that was lacking, or waning, about six years ago. I've met some really nice people online, who actually are what they seem when you finally get to meet them in person, and have expanded my author base quite considerably. I hope it has also made me more aware and compassionate towards everyone I come into contact with whether they are straight or gay.

◆　　◆　　◆

Ally

It definitely has. I've always believed in equality for all people, and I've always been a person who tended to agree with socially progressive politics. But since I've been involved in writing gay romance, I've actually become actively involved in socially progressive politics. Most of the things I've done have been under my real name, so I won't detail those actions here. But I've become involved in the fight for the defeat of DOMA and the defeat of Amendment One here in NC (which I hope will be history once this book is published), and all those things have directly led to my ongoing activity in the fight against the Republican war on women. Sorry if that's offensive to anyone, but there is a war on and women are literally fighting for our lives. I won't sugar-coat that.

So, there you go. I've always tended to be rather a rebellious and politically motivated person, but I think writing gay romance has made me an actively rebellious and political person. Whether that's a good thing or a bad thing depends on which side of the fence you're sitting on, I suppose :)

I vote good thing. So tell me, do you honestly believe one straight woman reading Gay Romance can make a difference in the world?

If reading gay romance leads that woman to become involved in the fight for equality, then yes, it's made a difference. Some people might say a single voice couldn't possibly change anything, but change comes from single voices joining together into a force to be reckoned with. So, yeah. Every voice counts. Gay romance brought me into the fight, and I suspect it brought a lot of other women in as well. That can only be a good thing.

◆   ◆   ◆

Kris

Oh totally. I never would have seen myself where I am now if it wasn't for the genre. If someone had asked me ten years ago if I wanted to be an editor (never mind the Executive Editor for a press), I would have laughed. As I've grown as an editor, I've gained confidence in other areas of my life. Would I have gotten to where I am personally without the genre, maybe. But I know that a lot of my self-confidence has been strengthen by coming to value what I bring to the genre. As a military spouse, raising two daughters (by myself for chunks of time), I can't be one to sit in the corner and wring my hands together—so I've always had some confidence but I find now that I share that more with my daughters as they see me face new challenges and achieve goals.

Most days I'd say I don't bring much to the genre; I'm just the editor, I don't write the words; and then I'm smacked upside the head virtually by one of my friends and I'm better. Or I get an email from one of my authors thanking me for working so hard with them on their story to make it a stronger story.

The genre has brought so much to my life that I'm glad that I'm a part of it.

◆   ◆   ◆

Stephani

Steph, has reading and writing Gay Romance changed the woman you are?

I would like to think it's made me a better mother and advocate.

Do you think one straight woman reading Gay Romance can make a difference to gay rights in the world?

Yes, I do. There are so many out there who don't know the very basic civil rights that are denied to gay men. Things like, marriage equality, housing and employment rights, DOMA and the fact that gay men can't donate blood. It's only by educating others that we can highlight how wrong this is and make a change.

◆　◆　◆

Lynn

Reading gay romance has made me very aware of the many issues that gay people must deal with all the time, everyday, everywhere! It's made me a cheerleader for gay rights and same sex marriage!! It's made me understand a little bit better what a gay person has to put up with from society, just because they love someone. My son is gay, I don't want him to feel he has to hide who he loves.

◆　◆　◆

Jen

Boy, I think I could write a book to answer this one! I have much more sympathy for LGBT people in general, and gay men in particular. Enough that I started volunteering. My heart breaks for those teens thrown away by their families for being gay, and I wish I could grab them all and give them a home and lots of love, because I have enough for all of them. But that isn't practical, unfortunately.

I've made some wonderful LGBT friends over the last four years, all of whom I would not have met if not for reading gay stories. My first great experiences were online with gay, male romance authors. I wrote some of them gushing about how I loved their stories and actually received answers from them. I was amazed at how friendly everyone was, and this is how I actually had my first story published. Once I started writing, I received wonderful support and mentoring from some of these same authors, such as A.J. Llewellyn, D.J. Manly, Neil Plakcy, and Patric Michael, all of whom I could ask about anything and get the answers I needed—in great detail, sometimes (Patric's essay on prostates is famous in some circles). I can't tell you how much I value their friendship and support as I grow as a person and writer.

When I attended the first Gay Romance Literature retreat in 2011 in New Orleans, I met even more amazing authors (like Geoff!), many of whom were women, and felt like I actually fit in somewhere at long last. Here is a group of like-minded people who love the genre as much as I do, and boy, is it a wonderful feeling! I feel like an odd duck sometimes in the rest of my life, particularly when my husband just cannot understand why I'm driven to do this, and need to spend so much time with my gay friends. It's like they get me so much more than my straight friends, and I love them all dearly.

Reading gay romances also allowed me to get a glimpse of a world where there were still unequal rights, and that made me passionate about marriage equality and LGBT issues, which were being fought in my own state. Sure, Massachusetts was the first U.S. state where same-sex marriage was accepted (and I'm damned proud about that), but transgender people were still having a terrible time with basic human rights. LGBT people have it more difficult in some ways, and reading gay romances opened my eyes to a lot of what I took for granted. I can get married to whomever I want, because I'm straight. I can have children and not have monstrous legal issues if we divorce or one of us dies, because I'm straight and legally married. I can see my husband in the hospital with no problem, because I'm his officially-recognized wife. I use my husband's medical plan because I'm married to him. We can file our tax returns together because we're married. Et cetera, et cetera.

Because I felt this was so wrong in so many ways, I made some major changes in my life by starting to do volunteer work in the gay community. It was working through MassEquality to help EqualityMaine defend its right to marry back in 2009 where I met and befriended my first gay couple, who became very close friends. The two men were married by their church in Maine, and were fighting hard to have it legally recognized. It was a sad day when it failed to pass, but we're all working for its passage this year. They introduced me to their gay men's group and I made more gay friends. I even spent a couple of evenings questioning the group about sex in real life, how they meet men, is there such as thing as a ménage, what about rimming, and other equally important questions that every (female) gay romance author wants to know. I think my friend gets a kick out of introducing his best friend Jonathan who writes gay romance, and seeing their shocked faces when a middle-aged woman enters the room. Not that I don't love it too. LOL

When I first started writing, I had to grab a pseudonym fast because I was job-hunting at the same time. I was afraid to tell anyone what I was doing and was very careful to keep real life and writing separate. Hence the male pseudonym. However, I found that my employer is very accepting and my manager and co-worker listen to me talk about my other life as a gay romance author and are very supportive. I've been involved in the diversity work at the office too and have made some fun friends in the LGBT community at work. They all know about my secret life and accept me with all my idiosyncrasies.

Probably my proudest moment, though, is when my daughter changed her viewpoint from being embarrassed about her mom's "gay porn stories," and started doing reports on gay issues and participating in her gay-straight alliance group in high school, continuing that support in college. She actually told her friends about what I was doing, including the volunteering, especially for Greater Boston PFLAG, and introduced me to some of them because they actually wanted to meet me. She worked in retail over the summer and now one of her best friends is gay. She told me just before she headed off to college that she now understood why most of my close friends are gay. "Mom, gay men are so much more fun!" That pretty much says it all!

◆　◆　◆

Dolorianne

Dolorianne, has Gay Romance made you into a different person?

Just more aware. I have gay friends, but it is definitely not the same as being gay. I am horrified at how some people are treated, usually by their own families, in these books, but I know it is nowhere near the physical and mental scars of the real people these stories represent. Luckily, none of the people I actually know went through anything too drastic when they came out, but that doesn't mean that stuff hasn't happened along the way that they would just rather not talk about. Having this insight allows me to view a situation or response I may have previously considered an overreaction, misunderstanding, or no big deal with more understanding and/or tolerance.

◆ ◆ ◆

Anne

Yes, absolutely. Then again, everything I read changes me—that's the reason I read in the first place (you should have seen how courteous and kind I was during my Jane Austen phase!). If a book doesn't change me, then I don't want to bother with it. So reading gay male fiction (as well as writing it) has made me more confident, more willing to stand up for gay rights as well as believe in them, and more willing not to run with the crowd when I think the crowd is mistaken.

Meanwhile, who knows what changes tomorrow will bring, but I'm looking forward to finding out!

◆ ◆ ◆

Carol

I've changed immensely in the years since I started writing. I used to live in a safe little box with only my own issues to deal with. Before I wrote my first story, I didn't even know blogs or Yahoo groups existed. I'd only inherited a computer a few months earlier and knew basically nothing about the internet. I think it was after I received my first contract that I learned I could actually talk to people online who enjoyed the same things I did. Pitiful, yes, but I think it's more common than a lot of people realize.

Carol, do you think one straight woman reading Gay Ro-

mance can make a difference to gay rights in the world?

A woman, who plants the seeds of tolerance in her children, fosters roots that will continue to spread and grow.

◆   ◆   ◆

CHAPTER THIRTEEN
CHILDREN OF THE REVOLUTION

I wanted to sign off on a similar note to Suzanne's introduction—the relationship between a mother and her gay son. After delving so deeply into the lives of these wonderful women, I needed to ask Lynn more about her relationship with her gay son and the impact it had on their family. I also wanted to learn more about Sheri's family and her open-minded attitude as to whether her son might be gay or not, something that only time will tell, but Sher-bear knows she will be there for him regardless of all else.

I also wanted to ask Norma about sharing her love of Gay Romance with her daughter, Emily. Norma and Emily aren't the only mother and daughter I've met who both enjoy Gay Romance, but is gay romantic and sexual content taboo for a parent and child, or does their common interest enhance their relationship?

After that I want to share with you two stories that I love, from two women I equally adore, both telling us their tales from a mother's point of view.

First up, Amelia from the world-famous Huffington Post will tell us about the first time her son said, "I'm gay." He was seven! And fearless! Because he knew no different.

And after that, gay romance author Stephani Hecht tells us about her son Cody, a young man who has become a true crusader for equality. Because not only are the straight women of this book a force to be reckoned with when it comes to love, acceptance and equality... there's a generation of kids out there like Cody and Jason and a million others who will be the children of a revolution.

Because we are indeed entering into a brave new world.

◆   ◆   ◆

Lynn

Lynn, after reading Suz's introduction on re-defining normal, do you think that your son redefined normal in the eyes of your in-laws because he was gay?

I think with my in laws, having a gay grandchild may have brought it closer to home for them. I mean here are two VERY conservative Christians, in their 70's, who are very much into what the Bible says. They live their lives according to what the Bible says. They believe that being gay is wrong, it's a sin, it's evil, you're going to hell if you're gay, etc... When my son was younger, my in laws took him to church with them, they paid for him to go to a private Christian school for nine years. And guess what, after all of that their grandson turned out to be gay. How ironic!

They may have had some talks amongst themselves, they probably even talked with their pastor. They've had some time to digest the news, because by the time we saw them again in person, they've had to accept that yes, they have a gay grandson. No matter what they've been taught and no matter what their Bible says, he's their grandson and they'll love him and accept him for who he is no matter what.

Has the relationship between you and your son changed since you started reading Gay Romance?

Not at all! We've always had a very open relationship with each other. Since he was little, I've always encouraged him to come to me with anything, so he's really comfortable talking to me about everything. He even tells me things that a Mom really doesn't need to know about their son! LOL

I asked him one time if he had a problem with me reading gay romance and he just said, "no, why would I have a problem with it"!

◆   ◆   ◆

Sheri

You have a 10-year-old daughter and a 13-year-old son. Will you ever tell them about your love of Gay Romance? Are you waiting for them to reach a certain age, is this something planned or are you just going to play it by ear??

This is a tough one. Maybe one day I'll tell them. I think I will just wing it for now, when and if the time is right. They both know I read romance, as they would say "lovey dove stuff, yuck..." They are too young for the wild crazy sex in most of these books, including most mainstream romances, too.

We just started the sex talk with my son and, oh, my god, how painful that was. After that, he showed some interest in a few gay websites. As any parent, I was floored that I found any porn on his computer at his age, but finding gay porn was a complete surprise. I was in shock for about a week and then I put my head back on my shoulder and closed my mouth.

In most of the gay romance, they always seem to have a lesson to be learned, or a moral to the story, I like that. I would definitely share my love of gay romance with him.

If your son turned out to be gay - and he may not - but if he did, I think he's the luckiest kid on Earth to have a mom like you who already has so much respect and interest in gay men..

Thanks, Geoff you are too sweet. You are right, we won't know if he is until he knows for himself. I love my son more than life itself and nothing can change that. As a mother, we are supposed to give our children the tools to help them in the world. When he is ready, he knows that I will be there for him no matter where it may take him.

◆   ◆   ◆

Norma

Norma, I've interviewed both you and your daughter, Emily, for this book. Some people might think that gay romance is a strange interest to have in common with your daughter. Is it?

What would you say to those people? Do you and Em discuss the books you read or are they just some things Mother and Daughter don't talk about?

I don't find it a strange interest to have in common with my daughter. Every day we have our own little mini book club where we discuss what we are reading and what we liked and didn't like about it... we have this game (I am thinking of a book) where we describe stuff in a book the other person gets to ask ten questions and have three guesses at the title. We talk about everything... I have always taught her – if you don't ask you will never know.

Okay, maybe we are not the normal mother and daughter duo, but at least we like each other having the same interests (though she glosses over the sex scene's I write because she doesn't want to think of me writing like that)... Cracks me up so I tell her in great detail sometimes, just to see her blush. It's the little things that amuse me sometimes.

◆   ◆   ◆

Amelia

I have always been a reader. Ever since I was old enough to pick up a book, I have been enthralled by the written word: Biographies, mysteries, collections of essays, romance, science fiction and fantasy, and stories of other cultures. Stories. That's what they all are, and we all have one. And I have one too.

This particular story started when my oldest son at the ripe old age of six years old fell in love for the first time. That first crush is a wondrous and adorable event—the smiles and blushes, the knowing this is the prettiest and talented person in whole wide world. It's one of those privileges of parenthood to watch it take root and bloom.

My son is a shy little boy, and on the first day of first grade he was having a hard time. The tears built up in his big eyes, as I kissed his cheek and squeezed his hand.

"I'll pick you up after school," I said and watched his eyes go even more glassy and nearly overflow. I got down to his level, took both of his hands, "You are going to have a great day. I am so proud of you." And with one last hug, I left before my eyes were as wet as his.

When I got to work I was a wreck. I made it to lunch somehow and to make myself feel better I spent the time writing out a short little story about my son and his crush. I wrote about how much I loved my child, and how I was glad he was my son. At my husband's insistence, I put it up online, on a blog I had never really used before. And that's where I thought the story would end.

But this is where it took a sharp turn. Within twelve hours my little story on my unknown blog had been shared more than 20,000 times, and that was just the beginning. People were fascinated by it, because my son's crush wasn't on a girl, but on a dapper gay boy on Fox's *Glee*.

The next few weeks were a whirlwind. Hundreds of LGBT children, as young as 14 years old, sent me messages thanking me for loving my own child...the way their parents didn't love them. Adults sent me heart wrenching tales of rejection by the families who loved them before they knew who they really were. Answering all my messages consumed me. There was so much pain, and these people were reaching out to me. The least I could do was reply. I wasn't going to be yet another person who ignored their pain.

I was asked to keep writing, not for my blog, but for the *Huffington Post*. It blew me away. I wasn't a writer. I was just me. When I got the man who would be my editor on the phone, I tried to explain to him that I wasn't "that mom." I don't bake, or even cook. I don't spend weeks planning elaborate children's themed birthday parties. I don't scrapbook or even see the point of keeping mementos around. I am a loud, brash, tattooed lady who has three kids. I work full time and my husband stays home. We live in the middle of the city, not a white-picket fenced suburb. All of these details didn't have the effect I was expecting: the editor saying, thanks for the call but you aren't who I thought you were, so we're going with someone else. It was the exact opposite. He loved it. He didn't want some ideal, he wanted a real mom, a real family. That was the story he wanted me to tell. Tattoos and all.

So, I started blogging for Huffington Post, even though I was still uncomfortable with it. The words of the kids who wrote to me were stuck in my head and in my heart. If these kids parents' wouldn't stand up for them, then I sure as hell could—especially with the support of my husband and my friends. I wrote for all those who saw hope in the story of our family. And after a while I could see how important our story was to people, and noticed everything I wrote had the same message: Hate isn't good for anyone and love is much more fun. And that was something I could get behind.

Eventually (at a wizened 7 years old) our son started identifying as gay. A lot of people think this was a brave statement for him to make, and I guess it is, but my son doesn't think so. LGBT people are a big part of our lives, important members of our friends and family. Homophobia has never been a value of our family. My sons have always known some of their favorite men are married to other men. They don't blink an eye that the little girl down the street has two mommies. It is beautifully normal to them. I can say with confidence that my 7 year old wasn't making a political statement, or even saying something he thought would make waves. He was simply describing himself the best way he knew how.

But as un-amazing as it might be to him, it did leave my husband and I grasping at straws. We had a first grader who identified as gay, and we had no reference, no touchstone. With most issues of parenting, there is somewhere to turn. If we had trouble potty training, there are innumerable books we could read or other parents we could go to for support. But this? Not so much. When I visited our local LGBT center and asked if there were any services, clubs, etc. for gay kids, I was told there were... for children 14 and up. And when I said, "My son is seven," I was met with what was becoming a familiar blank stare. They had never heard of a child that young "coming out." So, there we were. The parents of a son who announced proudly and happily he was gay. And we had no reference to turn to. So, we decided to do the only thing we could: let our hearts guide us. We love our kid. We love who he is. Our job as parents was no different, we would just keep doing the best we could, and let him know he is perfect exactly the way he is.

I might have been hopelessly naive when I posted my first blog, but I wasn't any more. I knew this blog could mean a lot to many people, but it would infuriate just as many. My husband and I talked about it extensively. Would I write about it? Should I write about it? If I did, how would I go about it? The discussion went on for over a month before we decided, yes, we would keep telling the story of our family. I would tell it as openly and honestly as I could, let come what may.

In my mind ours is a love story. The innocence of a first crush and first love. The love of a mother for her child. The family who tries to love each other for who they are. At its core it isn't a new story, or a perfect one, but it's ours…and I have come to realize, like all stories, it needs to be told.

◆   ◆   ◆

Stephani

Like most other mothers, I love my children and think that they are perfect in every way. They are my pride and joy, my reason for living, my greatest accomplishments ever. Yes, I may be a bit biased since they do belong to me, but I can't help but think that they are the best gift I could ever ask for. I know that I'm not the only one who feels that way about their kids, either. One look at the internet will show countless sites and blogs that highlight the many parents who are equally as proud and how deep their love for their offspring runs.

So how does a parent react when they are suddenly faced with the harsh reality that there are many in the world who hate their child? To the point where they not only say the most vile things against your offspring, but even go so far as to actually wish for the death of your kid? To make things even worse, if that were actually possible, they do this, not because of something said child had purposely done. No, it's all because of the simple fact that your child was born gay.

That is what we went through with our son, Cody. Or perhaps, I should point out it's what we *continue* to go through. As parents of a gay child, we have seen some of the worst society has to offer. The worst part is this battle is long from being over and we know it won't get any easier. At least for a while.

To put this all into perspective, we have to back up a couple of years. Cody was a junior in high school and looking forward to someday working in the health field. The career choice didn't surprise us since Cody has always been a caring individual. So much so, that when he turned seventeen he was excited that he could finally donate blood. He went to the first blood drive he could find and proudly displayed his sticker. Cody was also a member of the ski team, an avid mall rat and he was one of the few kids who actually enjoyed school. In short, he had it all, popularity, the ability to enjoy a life free from discrimination and the love of his entire family.

Then one day, two simple words changed all that, "I'm gay."

I wasn't surprised by the declaration. Looking back, that was one of the reasons I started writing M/M romance in the first place. Honestly, I think I'd been aware for several years and was just waiting for Cody to be ready to come out. So, when he did it was a big relief to both of us. We were finally able to get rid of the big, rainbow colored elephant in the middle of the room and start a new chapter in our lives.

Then came the disheartening revelation that one of my children, who I love more than anything in the world, was now going to be treated like a second-class citizen. Remember how excited he was about being able to donate blood? That was no longer a possibility. Right after he came out, we attended the wedding of my cousin. The entire time all I could think about was how the government refused to allow my son to have a marriage of his own. Then came the startling revelation that in our home state of Michigan, he could be fired or denied housing, just because of his sexuality. That was only a taste of what we now as a family had to deal with.

Every day we are faced with hate—hate that is directed at our baby. Let me tell you, nothing hurts a mother more than to see somebody attacking their child. There have been two times now where so-called churches or pastors have approached my son and told him he was going to hell. I ask myself how these men could be so cold-hearted as to attack a teenager and say such mean things? Where is the divine love in that?

Believe it or not, as horrible as all this is, Cody is one of the lucky ones. He has the full support of my husband and I, my sister and her husband, plus both sets of grandparents. Sure, there were some in our extended family who didn't approve of his "gay lifestyle" (Ack! I despise that term!), but since we didn't approve of their hateful words and bigotry it was easy to write them out of our lives. After all, Cody didn't have a choice, he was born gay, but they chose to hate.

All this did make me want to do something to make a change. No, better yet, it gave me a burning desire to make a difference. Since I'm an author and our best weapon is words, I decided to put that tool to good use. I became an advocate, not only in my books, but in my everyday life. If Cody can be brave enough to come out of the closet, then I can be brave enough to stand out there and fight for equality.

As such, I now gear my blog and Facebook page toward highlighting LBGTQ issues and victories. I also started the Safe Reading Zone (safereadingzone.com) which is an outreach site for those in the LGBTQ community who may feel alone. Not only does the site have uplifting videos on it, but there are links to help sites from all over the world.

I know these are just small steps, but I like to think that they do some good. Even so, they don't even begin to compare to what Cody has already done in the short time since he came out. He started the first ever Gay, Straight Alliance at his high school, despite some heavy opposition from school administrators. He has also counseled many of his peers and helped them in their own journeys. He even changed his college major. He is now working toward a degree in Public Administration so he can someday work for a non-profit LGBTQ organization.

People often say that Cody is lucky to have me as his mother. While I appreciate their kind words, I want to point out that I'm the lucky one. I have a child who is beautiful on the inside and out. He is so brave, so wonderful, so compassionate, so smart, so driven, so accomplished—in short he's every mother's dream. There is not one thing I would change about him, especially the fact that he's gay.

Sure, it will mean that he will face many battles in life, but I am determined that he won't be alone. I will be standing right next to him the entire way and I refuse to give up until he has every right he deserves. I also hope that my books will highlight the issues LGBTQ people face every single damn day. That way maybe more people will see how wrong things are and stand up for what is right.

◆ ◆ ◆

ONE MAN'S GOOD, TWO ARE BETTER
LAURA BAUMBACH

Passion. Lust. Strength. Dominance. Power. Tenderness. Submission. Wonder. Anguish. Overwhelming love. That's what hit me when I read my very first m/m erotic fiction. I never imagined it would be such a turn on!

It was a piece of fanfiction (fanfic) written by an author with the pen name of Molly Schneider. I was bowled over with the writing, the emotions, the level of intimacy and passion in the story. I became addicted in the first few thousand words. That was thirteen years ago.

I hadn't been looking for slash fanfic, heck, I didn't even know it existed. I had only recently found fanfic on the net and had finally moved from making my dear husband find stories for me (being internet stupid at the time) to looking for them on my own. I was following a TV series called *Forever Knight*, a vampire/detective story. I loved the characters and the love/hate relationship between the young vampire and his creator, an older, harsher vampire. I saw it as more of a father/son or older brother/younger brother relationship with a lot of veiled angst and emotion. I think the mystery of the relationship, the parts that weren't shown on the show, were what intrigued me. The characters had been together over 900 years, under every possible circumstance. Their affection and devotion, even when the young man was trying to pull away, was more intense than any I'd seen before. It was compelling and more than a little mysterious.

Right up until I read Molly Schneider's stories. Then the light bulb came on!

Wow, the twist to lovers suddenly made the whole relationship make sense. All the pent up anger and passion was just amazing. The love scenes in the fanfic stories were thrilling, titillating, and sensual. A whole new passionate world opened up to me.

It was wonderful, safe, to be on the outside looking in to the relationship. No games, no worry about pregnancy or loss of respect if you slept together on the first date. No girl problems! Just hunky men loving each other. The power and passion were overwhelming.

I read everything in the slash world I could, frustrated when I found more terrible stories than excellent ones. Not that that kept me from reading them, it just gave me a greater appreciation for the good stories peppered in among the foul. But it got harder and harder to find stories that gave me that same rush of excitement and satisfaction that Molly's stories had given me. I branched out to reading different series hoping to find more quality reads but, they too, soon dwindled. So I took the big leap—I wrote my first fanfic and eventually my first m/m erotic romance. I was writing m/m before it was even called that and before epublishers were releasing it. Thank you, fandom!

My first slash fanfic (or m/m erotic romance) came about when I was involved as a medical consultant on an independent script being produced starring one of the actors from a series I enjoyed and wrote non-slash fanfic for. This was twelve years ago. It was about modern day vampires and the possible medical cause behind the transformation. I was intrigued, as a medical professional, by the premise and enjoyed the characters. Since the California producers were fanfic writers themselves, they encouraged people to write fanfic about their characters. I jumped on board immediately.

I was lured into the myth of the script's premise by intense play of emotions between the two male leads, an ancient vampire captured for medical study and a young doctor who was drawn into the project by conniving men. The chemistry between them sizzled, even in the script that had been written for the general audiences. I couldn't wait to take the relationship to the next level. I wrote ten novellas based on the story line. Each one became more intense, more physical, and more passionate as I gave my creativity permission to write what I was feeling, what I wanted others to see in the relationship. I took the 'buddy' relationship to the next level and made them lovers. I imagined dark, intriguing, passionate love scenes interlaced with heartfelt words of love from the dramatic, worldly vampire that were meet with angsty but eager responses from the young doctor. I wrote about the human drawn into the dark world of vampires to safeguard his own life but who remained for love and passion.

I'll admit that in the beginning I was a bit restrained in my writing of the love scenes, but because I didn't feel able to write about sex between two men, but because I wasn't confident my writing was good enough for others to read it. The fanfic world is huge, made up of hundreds of thousands of readers and writers. I was shy about my work being read and valued. That changed when the producers of the movie asked to publish my body of fanfic for their characters and the response from bookstores and distributors was to ask for more. More work, more original characters and more writing from—ME.

So I wrote three novels, one right after the other, *A Bit of Rough*, *Out There in the Night* and *Details of the Hunt*. Contemporary lovers, werewolves and space pirates. I truly let my imagination have free reign. And the sex scenes practically made the pages spontaneously combust. They were met with approval from readers.

Fan mail started coming in, the first letter from a male reader. I was surprised—and enormously pleased—by the fact he enjoyed my work. He commented I handled the sex scenes pretty well. As a medical professional with an adventurous sex life of my own, I think I have a lot bases covered from real life experiences. Oral sex, hand jobs, kissing, anal intercourse—straight women do those things, too! He was surprised I was a woman. I was surprised he found my writing hot and enjoyable.

The biggest surprise was that the vast majority of my fan mail started coming in from straight women. Women who admitted they had been reading gay erotica for years, sometimes, decades, for the intense encounters, they offered. Gay erotica filled a need they were looking for but they were finding m/m erotic romance more satisfying by leaps and bounds. Now their stories not only had passionate sex but great characters, a solid plot and romance! *Real romance*, not just sex. Suddenly I realized that I wasn't the only straight woman out there reading m/m romance. Not the only straight woman by any means!

There were a large number of straight women writing slash fiction. If only one in five hundred who enjoyed it actually sat down and wrote it, there were tens of thousands of women out there looking for a more satisfying read. They were looking for m/m romance and m/m erotic romance.

It was reassuring to know not everyone out there would look at me like I was a three-headed monster when I told them what I wrote beyond mentioning it was romance. Yes, most people I mentioned it to, usually coworkers at the hospital, gave me a funny look and dropped the subject. One insisted she would pray for me. Well, hell, I guess someone should. Not for my writing but just on general principle. I have a family that long ago learned I was open and straightforward about everything I did, including my writing. I also worked at a hospital in the Northeast where discrimination wasn't a factor I had to deal with in regard to my job security because of the category of romance I wrote in. Not every author is as fortunate.

Occasionally, someone would want to know more. A woman sitting beside me on a flight to Romantic Times convention during one of the early years asked me what I did. I told her and we had a nice conversation for several minutes. Silence fell for a few more minutes then she leaned over and said, "I must have misheard you. What did you say you wrote?" I explained again in more detail and by the end of the flight she had asked for my business card and website. She was a lawyer on her way to do business in Washington, D.C. Some people realize they are interested in the m/m category of romance only once they know it exists. It's like finding your new favorite ice flavor. A personal indulgence that makes you happy.

Learning to write, even fanfic, took time, experience and the help of several gracious and learned beta readers. It became all consuming during my free time. The m/m category of erotic romance became my Mecca. It called to me. I'd start writing a mainstream story and then sudden the characters would shift. The female character became a secondary character and the two males in the story—there were always at least two males for some reason—would take over and eventually become the romantic pairing. It's not possible to write a male/female paring than just go in and change the female to a male. That's called 'chicks with dicks' in our world. The whole dynamic changes when it is two men, the responses, change the dialogue changes. After a while, I stopped even adding in the female component unless the plot called for it. The m/m romance and intimacy became my sole focus. I worked hard, wrote continuously and established a small but loyal following.

I soon shifted to writing original characters exclusively. I expanded beyond the small publisher who published my collection of fanfic and began submitting to other ebook publishers. I was eventually published by five separate houses. I was thrilled to be reaching so many readers!

But stumbling blocks were coming my way.

While the publishers and readers welcomed me, reviewers and writing contest sites did not. It became a daily battle to find a recognized review site that would accept m/m erotic romance for review. Without reviews, a writer's work reaches a limited audience. I wrote and submitted and questioned site coordinators with little to no success. Naïve to the romance community workings, I couldn't believe that my category of romance was being left out in the cold.

My work was just as good as my peers who wrote mainstream erotic romance. I had validation with writing awards with both fanfic and screenwriting manuscripts before I came to romance. I earned recognition from my publishers and had readers asking for more. I couldn't accept that stories in the m/m category weren't judged on the same standard as other romances. It became my mission to help level out the playing field.

The Romance Writers of America (RWA), of which I am a member, had accepted the definition of romance as a love story between two people. Not a man and a woman but two people. If the organization that set the standards for the romance community accepted it why weren't the supporting pegs in the industry doing the same?

Even the Romantic Times (RT) magazine, the main romance industry avenue for romance writer's work to be heralded, won't review the category. I've spent thousands of dollars on ads with them and at their yearly conference, struggling to be recognized as a legitimate part of the romance industry. I even became a member of their Fairy Fall court one year because it guaranteed a review of one book by all members. Not a guaranteed good review but an honest review. I submitted my book *A Bit of Rough*—a m/m because that's all I write—and it was rejected. I wasn't trying to pay for a good review, an honest review was all I was hoping for like everyone else that submits to them for review. I had submitted it before for review with no luck but, I was hoping spending *twelve hundred dollars* to be a member of their court would finally open the door. I was wrong. Let's just say after a long and unpleasant interaction they held to their point of view that there was no audience for the romance category with their readership so there was no point in representing it. My standing was if they were presenting themselves as THE review magazine for the romance community they should represent the entire community, including m/m romance and not just take money for advertising from its authors. It's an ongoing issue.

That was the start of a long string of interactions and efforts to break down a few doors. In 2012, *after ten years* of working to make this happen, RT Magazine did a five page article on the rise of m/m romance. Congratulations, RT!

While I was battling the system, communication from readers was coming in at a fairly steady pace. I began to see how important these stories were to both the gay men and the straight women reading my work. Not just the enjoyment factor or the titillation of the erotic content. These stories meant so much more to many of them. The email that hit me the most was from a young man who talked about how he got so caught up in the romance between Bram and James in my story *A Bit of Rough*. He dreamed of finding a personal relationship like the two characters had and thanked me for writing. That part was a common theme from readers but the next thing he said brought tears to my eyes. He said his mother had given him the book after she read it. She wanted him to have a man like Bram in his life one day.

This was a mother's hopes and dreams for her child.

I was stunned at how my stumbling attempt to write a simple story to see if I could actually create original characters people would like had touched another's life in such a deep and meaningful way. As the mother of two sons, I could relate.

Yes, these are fictional characters that don't exist. But if I have done my job right, they are fully fleshed out men with strengths *and* flaws, capable of being real living, breathing people. Any romance character, whether mainstream, m/m or any part of the GLBT category, are the incarnation of what people hope for in their lives. They fulfill that part for romance readers that is reaching for something passionate and exciting, whether it is just in their fantasies or something they aspire to have in their real life.

It was at this point I became totally dedicated to the m/m romance category. Fourteen books later and I can't tell you how many short stories, I still write only m/m erotic romance.

Seeing that m/m authors needed a voice in the reviewing and advertising world, I creating a co-op of authors to pool resources and buy larger advertising space in magazines, newspapers, and websites. We sponsored booths at big ticket events like BookExpo America and American Library Association conventions. We attended Leatherfests, Gay Pride Events, Romantic Times conferences, RWA conferences and any place I could find a spot where we could raise our profile, where readers and the powers that be could see we were here and here to stay.

RWA, our parent organization, puts a lot of emphasis on print books and being on bookstore shelves. Getting our work into print was much more difficult than mainstream romance. We sold very well in ebook format but few publishing house that did ebooks also did a lot of print and many weren't willing to take the chance on putting m/m into print. Most assumed that only gay men were reading the category. It wasn't a market they worked in and few would consider the value of entering the GLBT advertising avenues. What they didn't realize was they already marketed to the biggest audience for m/m—straight women.

Late in 2006, I took a long hard look at what I thought the m/m romance category needed. There were two things that stood out to me. First, we needed our books in print. Not just a few but, all of them. If they were good enough for ebook they were good enough for print or they shouldn't have been published at all. Secondly, we needed a voice in the RWA to gain recognition as a legitimate category within the industry.

The solution to the print books was easy. Well, that's what I said in 2007 when I decided to open my own publishing house, ManLove Romance Press, LLC aka MLR Press. It proved to be far from easy but, we're still here six years later and we aren't going anywhere any time soon.

I retired from nursing, put my heart and soul (and my retirement fund) into what I believed in and this became my life. Along with my top-notch, powerhouse Executive Editor Kris Jacen and highly gifted Head Graphic Artist Deana C. Jamroz, we have publish over one hundred twenty gifted authors in the m/m and gay fiction categories. Every full length story goes to print and is available for any bookstore in the USA and abroad.

We are on bookshelves! In the book world that translates to 'We are legitimate and important. We have arrived'.

Next was establishing a voice in the industry. I'm proud to say that a few years later, I helped found a new special interest chapter in RWA. The #217 Chapter of the Romance Writers of America, the *Rainbow Romance Writers*, was started with the hard work of the first group of officers, Jade Buchanan, J.L. Langley, and Kimberly Gardner. This is one of my biggest achievements. It gives voice to our category within the parent organization and allows us to be a recognized part of the romance industry.

It means everything to me to have our category acknowledge

by the book buying world, by RWA and by review sites. It means we are on equal ground with the rest of the romance community. It's what I have worked for for over twelve years. I've weathered insults, disappointments, setbacks, and even threats to get to this fair place. M/M readers and my family have always stood by me, which was my comfort and strength.

It was especially sweet when *Rolling Stone Magazine* declared M/M romance the topic of the year in their October 2010 issue under *WHAT'S HOT in Paperbacks* and I was named 'a premier author of M/M romance'. I never expected to see my name in a mainstream magazine, let alone Rolling Stone. I have it framed and hanging on the wall over my desk. Right next to that young man's letter.

I don't dismiss the original reason I wrote and read m/m erotic romance. I love the hot sex, the handsome men fighting to be with one another against the odds, the more equal power dynamic and the thrill of being on the outside looking in. One man's good, two are better. Those things still motivate me along with the chance to make a difference to my readers and to other m/m authors.

They are the reasons I continue to write and publish m/m. They remind me that it is worth all the struggle, sacrifice, insults and threats. I am a straight woman who writes m/m romance for other straight women and gay men and it matters. It matters to them and to me. Everyone deserves a happy ending—in their fantasies and in real life.

◆　　◆　　◆

DE-CODING THE LANGUAGE
WHAT WERE THEY SAYING?

Did it seem like we were talking another language occasionally? If you came across a few acronyms or terms you're not familiar with, hopefully this list will help explain a few things.

BDSM: Sexual scenarios involving Bondage, Discipline, Domination/submission, and/or Sadism/Masochism

DADT: Official U.S. military policy Don't Ask, Don't Tell, repealed on Sept 20, 2011

DOMA: The Defense of Marriage Act defining marriage as a union between a man and a woman

Fanfic: Fiction written by fans involving characters already created and published

Gaydar: Colloquial term referring to an intuitive ability to sense whether someone is gay or not

GFY: Gay For You, referring to a heterosexual character in a story finding love in a monogamous homosexual relationship

GRL: GayRomLit, an annual retreat for readers, writers and publishers of Gay Romance

HEA: Happily Ever After, referring to the happily ever after end of a romance story

HFN: Happy For Now, referring to the ending of a romance story that is not quite Happily Ever After, but still has a positive outcome

M/F/M: A romantic and/or sexual relationship between three people—a man, a woman and another man, where the two men don't engage in a sexual relationship with each other just with the woman.

M/M: A romantic and/or sexual relationship between two

men

M/M/F: A romantic and/or sexual relationship between three people—two men and a woman, where the two men do engage in a sexual relationship with each other and the woman.

MC: Main Character

NOLA: New Orleans, Louisiana

POV: Point of view

PWP: Porn Without Plot

RL: Real Life

Slash: Fan fiction with a main focus on sexual content, generally where the main characters are both male

Yaoi: Japanese fiction and/or art featuring homoerotic or romantic content specifically aimed at a female audience; also known as Boys' Love.

CONTACTS
HOW TO FIND THE
PEOPLE IN THIS BOOK

We've started the discussion on to Why Straight Women Love Gay Romance, but this is just the beginning. If you want to know more—if you're curious or puzzled or interested in digging a little deeper—most of those involved in this project were willing to include their contact details for anyone who'd like to share their views or ask more questions.

So if you're intrigued to know more, please ask away!

Geoff

www.geoffreyknightbooks.com

Kris

KrisJacen@mlrpress.com

Ally

www.allyblue.com

Amelia

www.huffingtonpost.com/Amelia

Amy

www.mantasticfiction.wordpress.com

Anke

anke_gabriel@yahoo.com

Anne

www.annebrooke.com

www.gayreads.co.uk

albrooke@me.com

Carol

www.carol-lynne.net

Dawn

www.dawnsreadingnook.blogspot.com

www.loveromancesandmore.blogspot.com

Dolorianne

www.mantasticfiction.wordpress.com

mantastic@live.com

Elisa

www.elisa-rolle.livejournal.com

Erica

www.ericapike.com

Helen

www.helenbeattie.com

helen@helenbeattie.com

J. Rose

www.jroseallister.com

Jen

www.jontreadway.com

jontreadway@comcast.net

Jet

www.jetmykles.com

Kimber

www.kimberlygardner.com

Laura

LauraBaumbach@mlrpress.com

www.laurabaumbach.com

Lynn

www.mantasticfiction.wordpress.com

Norma

www.normajnielsen.com

www.normanielsen.blogspot.com.au

P.L. Nunn

www.bishonenworks.com/

Petchie

perpetua2206@yahoo.co.uk

Poppy

www.poppydennison.com

Ro

www.outstandinggayfiction.blogspot.com

Sheri

www.mantasticfiction.wordpress.com

Stephani

www.stephanihecht.com/Home.html

stephanihechtauthor.blogspot.com/

Suzanne

Suzanne Brockmann is a PFLAG mom, and the New York Times bestselling author of fifty-one romance novels, including Born to Darkness, the first book in a new mainstream paranormal romance series that includes steamy m/m love scenes. She has also recently co-written and co-produced The Perfect Wedding, an indie feature-length romantic comedy movie with a hero and a hero. Visit her website at http://www.SuzanneBrockmann.com, find her on facebook at www.facebook.com/SuzanneBrockmannBooks, follow her on Twitter

@SuzBrockmann, and check out the movie's trailer at http://www.theperfectweddingmovie.com/trailer.html

Wave

www.reviewsbyjessewave.com

Z

www.zallorabooks.com

◆ ◆ ◆

FROM THE FACTS TO A LITTLE FICTION

From the paranormal to the whimsical, from the historical to the contemporary, there are countless styles and sub-genres in Gay Romance. Now, for those who are curious, or for those who are already fans, I thought I'd leave you with a Valentine's story of mine.

This is just one Gay Romance story amongst thousands. If you like it, then maybe there are more stories out there you'll enjoy as well. If you don't like it, maybe you'll enjoy someone else's Gay Romance tales more than mine, I don't mind. This short story is just an example of what's out there. It's not necessarily representative of the power of Gay Romance…

…but everything you've read in this book up to this point, is.

Enjoy.

Video Store Valentine

Geoffrey Knight

It was here… again!

That day!

The one day of the year when lucky lovers get even luckier and hopeless romantics become just that little bit more hopeless.

"Wow, you're a real downer," the stranger sitting next to me on the subway train said.

"Shit," I cursed myself and moved seats.

This happened several times a week. Not the moving seats part, but the part where I turn my own internal monologue into an *external* monologue and vocalize whatever's in my head without even realizing it. The doctor gave me some pills once but they knocked me out completely. Have you seen *My Own Private Idaho*? I'm pretty sure they were narcolepsy pills that doctor gave me. I woke up three days later to find myself sitting on Coney Island's Wonder Wheel with my face in a bag of sugar-coated peanuts and a brand new yin and yang tattoo on my right forearm. Random, I know. Needless to say I threw the pills away and decided to manage my condition drug-free. I found that writing things down often helped. It was a way of getting things out of my head via pen and paper rather than via tonsils and tongue.

Back on the subway I made my way past the commuters with their once-a-year bouquets and heart-shaped boxes of chocolates clutched proudly in their hands, and found myself another seat on the train. I pulled my notebook from my pocket. On the cover I had written *This notebook belongs to Cal Nichols* as though I were a third-grader, but I figured if I ever featured in another episode of

A Zombie at Coney Island, perhaps next time someone might rescue me from the Wonder Wheel and discover my notebook and return me home safely. In my mind that someone looks like Ryan Gosling. And if the good Lord above in all his infinite wisdom (and trust me, this'd be a wise move, Lord) would guarantee that Ryan Gosling was indeed my savior—swinging in front of me from a Ferris wheel, begging for my love—then by God I'll start praying right now!

But in the meantime…

I flipped open my own notebook to today's entry: my list of things that would make Valentine's Day bearable.

DVDs (nothing romantic!)

Chocolate (with nuts)

Chips (anything but salt & vinegar)

Slushie (*Blue Lagoon* flavor)

Pizza (supremo, no anchovies, extra cheese)

Pint of Ben & Jerry's (Chunky Monkey)

The plan was to phone up for the pizza once I returned from the video store with everything else on my list, which was why I was on the subway. I used to be able to walk to my closest video store, but in the last two years video stores started dying out faster than the dinosaurs. I know the world will always change, but sometimes it makes my heart sink a little.

I now had to take the subway to my nearest store and endure being called a 'downer' by perfect strangers. The truth is I'm actually quite an 'upper'. It may be all that sugar, but the buzz food helps keep my brain ticking when I have to get creative with my film-school assignments. Vampires and werewolves don't survive on salads, and neither do I.

I was thinking about my latest project—the story of a man who falls in love with a woman who's actually been transformed into an evil robot by a mad scientist, inspired by Fritz Lang's 1927 German expressionistic masterpiece *Metropolis*—as I left the subway and walked the block to Movie Mania.

When I walked through the door to the video store I was fully expecting to see the assistant manager Roger—who wore his geekdom with so much pride he had even written *Ramjet* under his name on his name badge—putting returns on the shelf. But as I looked up I was suddenly struck with fear.

"Oh shit!"

Roger was nowhere in sight, and as if some mad scientist was up to some diabolical trickery, the person stacking the shelves with returns was—

—the hunky part-timer named Taylor!

Instantly I began backing out of the store, but before I could reach the door, Taylor looked up at me and smiled, his teeth so perfect and white I was certain there was a robot underneath his human facade.

"Hey, how you doin'?" he asked merrily, his entire persona nothing short of charming.

"G-g-good," I stammered, my getaway gone. "Thanks so much for asking."

Thanks so much for asking?

Really, Cal?

Desperately wishing that Roger Ramjet had been working the night shift instead of Prince Charming, I hurriedly turned and took refuge in the classics section.

The store was empty but for me, Taylor and a leggy young blonde holding hands with her college-jock boyfriend in the new release aisle. Oh, and Bette Davis. I only now realized that Taylor was playing *All About Eve* on the in-store monitors.

Goddammit! The bastard just went from perfect to demi-god!

Well, that was my opinion anyway.

The leggy blonde didn't seem to see any kudos in Taylor's

choice to play a Bette Davis movie.

"What's this crap?" she whined to her boyfriend, squinting up at the screen above her head, like a mosquito trying to figure out God! "Is that an old Meg Ryan movie?"

"Concentrate, cookie-crumbs," her boyfriend said in between trying to suck the lips off her face. "Let's not spend all night here. I'm horny."

Suddenly the blonde spotted something shiny on the shelf and jumped up and out. "Oh muffin-hunk, what about this one?" she asked in a high-pitched baby voice that almost made me gag on the spot. "I looooooove this movie. It's soooooo romantic."

"Oh, pookie-buns, we saw that one twice at the cinema, remember?" the jock tried to reason. "Besides, we've already got a Kate Hudson movie."

"No, that's not Kate Hudson. That's Katherine Heigl. Oh pleeeeaaaase, muscle-cakes. It's Valentine's Day!" Suddenly her baby voice turned into a stripper voice in one very unnerving moment. "If you watch them with me I'll let you make a movie of your own. Starring me."

The boyfriend grabbed the DVDs, hurried to the counter and emptied the entire contents of his wallet looking desperately for his membership card and some cash. "We're in a bit of a hurry," he told Taylor who found the guy's card and started scanning the DVDs.

"Having a cozy night in for Valentine's, I see."

"I don't sit through rom-coms to get cozy," the jock whispered to Taylor, a suggestive smirk on his face.

Suddenly the blonde draped herself over her boyfriend's shoulder and smiled at Taylor. "We're gonna cuddle on the couch with popcorn."

"But not too much popcorn, right peach-pie?" said her boyfriend with a kiss, shoving everything back into his wallet and tossing Taylor a ten dollar bill without a second glance. "You wanna look good for the camera, don't you?"

"Oh, I love it when he tells me what to do," the blonde said to Taylor, pinching her nose to make a cute squirrel face. Suddenly she noticed Taylor's name badge. "Say, you've got the same name as that *Twilight* guy… although he's much cuter than you. Oh, no offense. It's just he's a movie star and all, you know what I mean."

"I know what you mean," Taylor shrugged good-naturedly, but the blonde was already back to begging in her baby voice.

"Oh snookie-balls, can we please get *Full Eclipse* too… or *Breaking Moon*… or whatever the hell the new *Twilight* movie's called?"

"No, booboo-boobs, we can't. We gotta go. Sailor Sam just ran the flag up the mast."

The blonde jumped up and down excitedly. "Oooh, seamen ahoy!"

With that, she and her boyfriend snatched their DVDs and raced out of the store.

As for me, after that I needed a fuckin' slushie!

I wasn't even certain that *Blue Lagoon* would be strong enough. At that point I was willing to take a chance on the strongest color preservative I could get my hands on! Anything to get me through this Valentine's Day!

I cut a beeline to the slushie machine, all too aware that it was only me and Taylor in the store now.

Breathing the same air.

Listening to Bette Davis elegantly bite and claw her way through *All About Eve*.

Getting older together by the second…which was kinda romantic in a weird way.

Quickly I filled my extra large slushie cup with *Speed Racer* Red. I grabbed chocolates and chips. I found my Chunky Monkey in the ice cream freezer. And as bravely as I could, I marched up to the counter to present perfect Taylor with my imperfect junk food fetish.

My booty scattered across the counter—except for the slushie which I had already started sucking on like a security blanket— I prepared to be belittled and scorned for my bad food choices, safe in the knowledge that in a little while I'd be home again, happily locking out those happy couples celebrating another Valentine's Day.

But all Taylor said when he saw my snacks was, "Awesome!" And quite enthusiastically, I might add. "But don't you wanna watch a movie with your junk food?"

"Oh," I said lamely, suddenly realizing I'd forgotten to actually pick a DVD.

"I can help you choose something your girlfriend might like," Taylor offered helpfully. "Maybe Jennifer Aniston's new movie. Or Reeese Witherspoon. You know people are raving about Sarah Jessica Parker's new rom-com… if you like that sort of thing."

I shook my head quickly. "I don't like that sort of thing. And I don't have a girlfriend. Nothing against girlfriends, I'm just not that kinda guy."

His lips twigged, just a fraction. Damn, he understood subtext, so he was smart too!

He glanced from me to the junk food and back again. "Are you telling me all those snacks are for you?" he asked. "Wow, you must have an amazing metabolism. Where do you put it all? You must burn it all off. I can tell you work out, right?"

It was true, I was indeed lucky that I didn't wear all that crispy, gooey, delicious crap like sacks of sugar tied to my hips. In fact, I was in pretty good shape for a junk-food-aholic. I always believed it had something to do with my weird condition, but I wasn't about to tell Taylor that. Instead I smiled and shook my head and answered, "No, I keep kinda busy with film-school."

Taylor's face lit up. "You go to film-school? That's awesome! I'm an actor… well, sorta. All I've done so far is an ad for pimple cream, oh and the part of 'Foolish Paper-Shredding Mailroom Boy' in a corporate video for the Department of Occupational Health and Safety. It was a non-speaking role, although I did have to scream in fear. But I know some day I'm gonna be a real actor."

"Like Taylor Lautner."

"No, I mean a *real* actor," he said quite seriously.

I smiled approvingly and thought to myself, *That blonde was so wrong. You're way cuter than Taylor Lautner.*

A shy grin spread across Taylor's face. "Excuse me?"

"I didn't say anything," I replied, gulping worriedly. "Did I?"

Taylor raised one eyebrow quizzically. "You just said I was way cuter than Taylor Lautner?"

Oh fuck! Oh Jesus!

I could feel the blood drain from my face.

"Did I really say that out loud?"

Taylor laughed gently. "Yeah, you did. Unless I've suddenly turned into Dr. Jean Grey from the *X-Men* movies and read your mind. Which, I have to admit, I've tried to do many times but never actually succeeded. So, based on my track record, I'd have to say yes, you really did say it out loud. Followed by, 'Oh fuck! Oh Jesus!'" he added… not so helpfully.

Knees are no good if they don't keep you up.

I struggled to keep mine from buckling altogether before managing to point at the monitor above Taylor's head in a desperate bid to change the topic as fast as possible. "I'll take Eve to watch."

The words came out in a panic, and although a great film filled with enough class and antagonism to stick it to Valentine's Day in the most appropriate way, *All About Eve* wasn't quite the movie I was after.

In fact, although I would never admit it to anyone, I actually had something of a soft-ish spot for Valentine's Day… in my own way. It wasn't the same soft spot that most other people have. I just liked to do Valentine's Day *my* way.

I didn't need a special someone or a dozen red roses or a candle-lit dinner.

I just needed to *not* have the whole thing thrown in my face.

I needed my list.

I needed my treats.

And I needed a movie that wasn't corny or formulaic, yet a movie where the hero fell in love in the end. Because despite my frustrating condition and my addiction to sugar and my left of center ways, deep down I'm something of a hopeless romantic.

And hopeless romantics always wish for some hope… hopelessly.

The sad fact was I had never looked someone in the eye and said, "Happy Valentine's Day."

"Good choice," Taylor was saying, teleporting me back to the real world like Kirk after a mission to a strange planet made entirely of styrofoam boulders. "I love *All About Eve*. Hey and I love your tatt too," he said, pointing to my forearm. "Yin and yang. The idea that opposites ain't so different. In fact, they need each other if they wanna get through this world."

He smiled, and by way of introduction he showed me his badge… like I'd never noticed him before. "My name's Taylor, by the way."

I held up my membership card with my name on it, like I was goddamn Agent Starling in *Silence of the Lambs* flashing an FBI badge… before I dropped it on the floor. "I'm Cal Nichols."

The bumbling idiot!

"Nice to meet you, Cal. I'll get the DVD out of the player for you. Then you'd better fasten your seatbelts," he said in a surprisingly good Bette Davis impression, crouching down behind the counter to eject the movie from the machine, "you're in for a bumpy night!"

"You're dead right about that, sweetheart!"

The words didn't come from Taylor's sweet voice.

They seemed to splatter against the side of my face in a spray of cheap whiskey.

I turned and saw a man in a balaclava glaring at me. I saw the gun in his hand pointed down at Taylor and I gasped in horror.

Where the fuck did he come from?

"Uranus," the robber answered angrily. "Now shut the fuck up!"

Shit, I did it again!

Instantly my slushie tried to flee, slipping from my trembling hand and splashing all over the floor in an explosion of mushy red ice.

Taylor quickly rose from behind the counter, the *All About Eve* disc spinning on his finger. "Take it easy, dude," he said calmly, both hands in the air. "You don't wanna hurt anyone here."

"Shut up and open the register!" the man said, jabbing the gun in Taylor's direction. "Put all the money in a bag! Now!"

Taylor opened the cash register and pulled out a handful of five and ten dollar bills.

"And the rest!" the robber demanded.

"There is no rest," Taylor shrugged. "Blame downloading, dude."

"Fuck!" The robber snatched the cash and noticed the door to the storage room just behind Taylor. He swung the gun in my direction and I gasped again. "You! Both of you! Get in there."

With a shove he pushed me behind the counter with Taylor before forcing both of us into the storage room at gunpoint.

The moment we were inside, the door slammed shut behind us. We heard the sliding of a bolt on the other side of the door, followed by the rustling of junk food packets and the sound of items being thrown into a plastic carry bag—*he's stealing my Chunky Monkey!*—followed shortly after by a loud thud.

"Shit!" Taylor whispered before quickly turning to me, genuinely concerned. "Are you okay? He didn't hurt you?"

"No, I'm okay," I answered, although the quiver in my voice made it known that I was understandably rattled. "We gotta call the cops."

"We can't," Taylor said. "There's no phone in here. Do you have a cell?"

"No. I'm kinda old-fashioned like that."

"Kudos to you, man," Taylor said, before adding, "Except for now."

"What about you?"

"Mine's under the counter."

"Well what do we do?"

Taylor took a deep breath, lined his broad shoulder up with the door and rammed himself into it.

His heroics were impressive, and if we were in a movie I would have gushed a little as the door burst open.

But the stubborn door didn't do any bursting at all.

It simply shook on its hinges.

I gave a little gush anyway.

Taylor tried again and again, until eventually he gave up.

"Is there some other way outta here?" I started looking around the small room and suddenly squealed like a girl at the sight of a man with a butcher's knife standing in the corner.

"It's okay, Cal," Taylor said, putting his hand on my shoulder to calm my nerves. "It's just an old cardboard cut-out of Ghostface from *Scream*." Taylor suddenly spun toward me with a wicked grin on his face and in his best Ghostface voice asked, "What's your favorite scary movie?" Suddenly he let out an ungodly scream.

I squealed again, clutching at my chest before panting, "Jesus Christ! Are you trying to give me a heart attack?!"

"Shit, I'm sorry," he muttered guiltily. "I was just showing you my Foolish Paper-Shredding Mailroom Boy scream. I love the *Scream* movies. I'm a total movie nerd, I can't help myself sometimes. I didn't really mean to scare you."

"Well you did!" I said, still trying to slow down my galloping heart. "And how are you possibly a movie nerd. I mean, you're so damn…" I decided not to finish my sentence.

"So damn what?"

"Forget it," I said, already having made a big enough ass of myself with my girly squeals. "Let's just figure out another way outta here."

"There isn't one," Taylor said.

At a glance I could see he was right. The walls were lined with shelves full of old VHS tapes and replacement DVD cases. There were a few old VHS and DVD machines stacked in one corner, along with an old TV set and a handful of movie posters rolled up with elastic bands.

But there was no other door and not a single window in sight.

"So what do we do?" I asked, panic rising in my voice. "What if we run out of air?"

Taylor took me by both shoulders this time, his grip on me firm and masculine. It took my breath away for a moment. "It's okay," he said. "There's plenty of air in here. And all the lights are on in the store and the sign on the door says we're open. We just gotta listen out for the next customer to come in, then yell for help like crazy. Of course, the way video stores are these days that could be a while. But someone will come, I promise you."

His voice was calming. He gave me a smile. "Feeling a little more relaxed?"

Actually, what I was feeling was my cock twitch and swell as Taylor stood there, holding me by the shoulders. I nodded before he squeezed his hands.

"Are you sure you don't work out?" he asked.

"Positive. The only thing I lift is my camera gear."

"That stuff can get pretty heavy. So that's how you stay in shape. Me, I have to drag my ass to the gym as often as I can."

"So I see," I said before I could help myself.

"Thanks," Taylor said, flattered. "You know what showbiz

is like. If you wanna be an actor you gotta look the part, right?"

Proudly—but in no way arrogantly—he flexed a muscle.

At the same time, the muscle in my jeans did some flexing of its own.

"Say, maybe you and me could make a movie together some day," Taylor said enthusiastically.

My hard-on grew into a harder-on as I recalled the conversation between the blonde and the jock.

Taylor must have noticed the look on my reddening face and thought the same thing. He quickly back-tracked, embarrassed. "No, I don't mean *that* kind of movie. I mean a real movie. With a script and everything."

My heartbeat hadn't slowed down at all. In fact, right now it was going faster than a bus with a bomb on board. But just like Sandra Bullock at the wheel of an out-of-control, twelve-ton vehicle, I suddenly felt both terrified... and brave. "I'd love to make a movie with you," I said with a gulp. "You'd make a great leading man."

"I would?" he asked excitedly.

"Of course you would. You're so damn..."

"So damn what? Just say it."

"Well, you're so damn... hot."

"I am?" He sounded surprised.

"Yes. You are. You don't see that?"

"Maybe. Not really."

This time it was Taylor's turn to blush. I didn't mean to embarrass him so I quickly said, "Or maybe you'd rather play a villain? You'd make a great villain!"

A damn sexy one!

The second I thought it, I knew it had come out of my mouth. "I just said that out loud too, didn't I?"

Taylor blushed even more, but he couldn't hold back his

smile. "You really think I'd make a sexy villain? You mean like Brad Pitt in *Thelma and Louise*?"

We were both blushing now. There was pretty much nothing more I could say to embarrass myself, so I finally started to relax. "He's more of a loveable rogue than a villain."

"And a much better armed robber than our friend tonight," Taylor added, seeming to relax as well. Suddenly he reached for one of the shelves, grabbed a price gun, held it up like a weapon and proceeded to do a damn good Brad Pitt southern drawl. "Ladies and gentlemen, who wins the prize for keepin' their cool? Simon says everybody down on the floor. Now, if nobody loses their head then nobody loses their head. You sir, you can do the honors. Take that cash, put it in that bag right there and you got an amazing story to tell your friends. If not, well, you got a tag on your toe. You decide."

Taylor ended his performance by stuffing the price gun into his jeans and winking at me. My heart swooned and before I knew it I was applauding. "Holy shit, that was great!"

"You think so?"

"It was totally awesome. Except that…"

"Except what?"

I hesitated. "Well, Brad Pitt does that scene without a shirt."

"Oh shit, you're right." Like a true actor rising to the challenge, Taylor started to pull his shirt off. Suddenly he stopped and asked, "Do you mind if I take my shirt off?"

"I don't mind at all," I mumbled dreamily.

Taylor smiled again. "Me neither."

He peeled off his Movie Mania polo shirt to confirm my fantasies of a six-pack stomach and perfect chest.

And all I could say was, "What are you doing working on Valentine's night? Aren't you supposed to be out on a date or something… instead of locked in a stupid storage room… with me?"

Taylor shrugged. "I guess I didn't feel like going out. Last week I got dumped by my boyfriend."

I swallowed so loud my throat clicked. "Your boyfriend?"

"Well, ex-boyfriend now. He said I wasn't 'cool' enough for him."

"What the fuck does he call 'cool'?"

Taylor shrugged again. "I dunno. Designer clothes, nightclubs with red carpets, hanging out with the in-crowd. I know I'm supposed to care about all that stuff, but I don't."

"That stuff's all bullshit. Nightclubs with red carpets are full of people with no talent. In-crowds are always on the way out. And what good are designer clothes gonna be if a zombie apocalypse happens, huh?"

"You're right," Taylor nodded. If I thought his perfect white smile couldn't get any bigger, I was wrong. "Cal Nichols, will you spend Valentine's night with me?"

If I thought my cock couldn't strain any harder against the inside leg of my jeans, well, I was wrong about that too. "Sure," my voice trembled.

"Cool!"

Taylor went to another shelf and grabbed a dusty old machine. He showed it to me like a kid with a new toy on Christmas morning and asked, "When was the last time you watched a VHS?"

Excitedly he put the machine on the floor before grabbing the old TV. He wiped the dust off the screen with his forearm, set it down next to the VHS player and began plugging plugs into sockets.

"Are you sure we should be watching a movie?" I asked. "Shouldn't we be listening out for customers?"

"We can do both," Taylor answered. "Trust me. I know the perfect movie. It's an old silent classic."

Suddenly he was climbing the shelves like Ethan Hunt on an impossible mission, his eyes scanning along the spines of old movies. As he inched across the shelves his sneakers slipped.

I caught him by grabbing his ass—which I'm happy to report was rock hard—and helped him regain his footing.

"Thanks," he said.

"No problem," I answered, reluctantly letting that ass scale higher up the shelves before he found what he was looking for.

I helped him down, guiding his feet from one shelf down to the next as I said, "It makes me sad, you know."

"What does?"

"What you said before. What we all know. That it might be a while before another customer comes along. That video stores aren't what they used to be. People forget what an icon they are. They're my childhood. Videos were my babysitter when I was growing up. They were my best friend. The world will never have this again. The video store can never be replaced. Like drive-in movies. And records with scratches on them. Once they go, we'll never get them back. And we'll wonder why we chose to turn them into memories in the first place."

Taylor stepped down off the last shelf, a VHS in his hand, and simply looked me in the eye. "That's the most romantic thing I've ever heard," he said.

I gulped. "Really?"

He nodded. "Really."

Suddenly his face was close to mine.

I could smell his sweet breath and realized he'd recently helped himself to a spoonful of his own Chunky Monkey.

And before I knew it, his soft lips were pressed against mine.

That's when I shut my eyes and saw it all:

Fireworks exploding!

Trains rushing through tunnels!

Daniel Craig coming out of the sea in *Casino Royale*!

Once again those knees of mine had to pull their socks up to do their duty as Taylor's lips parted; as his tongue pushed gently into my mouth; as the air escaped his nostrils in short bursts that warmed my upper lip.

He pressed his hips against mine and I could feel the bulge in his crotch rub against my hard-on.

I dared to lay my hand on his perfect bare chest, my fingers turning into ice-skates on his tanned skin, gliding swiftly down to his nipples.

I squeezed the tight buds in my fingertips.

Taylor let out a moan and bit down on my bottom lip.

Suddenly I needed air.

I pulled out of the kiss, dizzy and elated, but stayed close, not knowing what to say except, "What's movie did you pick?"

Taylor grinned. "A love story. About a guy who falls in love with a woman only to discover she's been transformed into an evil robot by a mad scientist. It's called—"

"—*Metropolis*," we both said at once.

I stared into Taylor's eyes.

He stared into mine.

And suddenly—

"Hello? Is anybody here? I'm calling the police!"

The muffled cry came from the other side of the door.

Taylor and I both ran for the door, pounding and shouting, "We're in here! Please help us, we're locked in the storage room."

After a moment we heard the bolt slide across and a stunned old man opened the door. "What's going on here?"

"Sir, everything's okay," Taylor said. "We were robbed."

"No shit, Sherlock! I come down here to rent some frilly French movies for Valentine's Day and end up walking into a crime scene!"

"What do you mean?"

The old man led us around to the front of the counter, where

I had been standing at the time of the robbery, and pointed down at the robber lying face-down on the floor, unconscious, his gun a few feet away.

"Looks like he slipped and knocked himself out," the old man said, pulling out his cell phone. "There's blood everywhere? I'm calling 911!"

"That's not blood," I said, kneeling beside the unconscious robber and slopping up a sample on the end of my finger, just like Agent Starling would. "That's *Speed Racer* Red!"

As the old man stumbled outside yelling into his phone to the emergency operator, Taylor knelt beside me, his eyes beaming. "You stopped the bad guy. You saved the day!"

"I did?" I asked. Then I nodded and smiled. "I guess I did."

Taylor took a deep breath and asked, "Cal, will you be my leading man?"

"Yes!" I thought out loud. Loud and proud. "Maybe we can finish our Valentine's Day without a guy with a gun."

"How does tomorrow night, sound? My place at eight o'clock. I'll bring *Metropolis*. But only on one condition."

"What's that?"

"You bring your camera." He kissed me again, a long, sweet, movie-star kiss, before adding with a wink, "Happy Valentine's Day, Cal."

And for the first time in my life I looked someone in the eye and said—

"Happy Valentine's Day."

◆　　◆　　◆

ABOUT THE AUTHOR

From palace-hopping across the Rajasthan Desert to sleeping in train stations in Bulgaria, from spinning prayer-wheels in Kathmandu to exploring the skull-gated graveyards of the indigenous Balinese tribes, Geoffrey Knight has been a traveller ever since he could scrape together enough money to buy a plane ticket. Born in Melbourne but raised and educated in countless cities and towns across Australia, Geoffrey was a nomadic boy who grew into a nomadic gay writer. When he's not travelling the world, Geoffrey is travelling the world of his imagination—where the adventures, thrills and romance are limitless.

He currently owns his own advertising and design agency which he runs from his island home on the Great Barrier Reef, and can't wait to buy his next plane ticket—whether it's real or imaginary.

Rainbow Romance Writers

Raising the Bar for LGBT Romance

RRW offers support and advocacy to career-focused authors, expanding the horizons of romance. Changing minds, one heart at a time. www.rainbowromancewriters.com

The Trevor Project

The Trevor Project operates the only nationwide, around-the-clock crisis and suicide prevention helpline for lesbian, gay, bisexual, transgender and questioning youth. Every day, The Trevor Project saves lives though its free and confidential helpline, its website and its educational services. If you or a friend are feeling lost, alone, confused or in crisis, please call The Trevor Helpline. You'll be able to speak confidentially with a trained counselor 24/7.

The Trevor Helpline: 866-488-7386

On the Web: http://www.thetrevorproject.org/

The Gay Men's Domestic Violence Project

Founded in 1994, The Gay Men's Domestic Violence Project is a grassroots, non-profit organization founded by a gay male survivor of domestic violence and developed through the strength, contributions and participation of the community. The Gay Men's Domestic Violence Project supports victims and survivors through education, advocacy and direct services. Understanding that the serious public health issue of domestic violence is not gender specific, we serve men in relationships with men, regardless of how they identify, and stand ready to assist them in navigating through abusive relationships.

GMDVP Helpline: 800.832.1901

On the Web: http://gmdvp.org/

www.ingramcontent.com/pod-product-compliance
Lightning Source LLC
LaVergne TN
LVHW011155080426
835508LV00007B/419